Offeri
Ken
Anglicanism:

Liturgical Texts and Contexts including 'A Kenyan Service of Holy Communion'

by

Graham Kings and Geoff Morgan

with a preface by

David M Gitari

GROVE BOOKS LIMITED
RIDLEY HALL RD CAMBRIDGE CB3 9HU

Contents

CONTRIBUTORS

Canon Graham Kings is the Vicar of St Mary Islington and a member of the Liturgical Commission of the Church of England. From 1985 to 1991 he was Director of Studies and Vice-Principal of St Andrew's Institute, Kabare, Kenya and from 1992 to 2000 was the Henry Martyn Lecturer in Mission Studies and the founding Director of the Henry Martyn Centre for the study of Mission and World Christianity, in the Cambridge Theological Federation, England.

Revd Geoff Morgan is an Academic Tutor and Taught Programmes Manager at the Oxford Centre for Mission Studies, Oxford, England. A teacher and a priest, he was most recently Associate Vicar of St Martin of Tours with St Stephen-on-the-Downs, Epsom in Guildford diocese.

ABBREVIATIONS

ACK	Anglican Church of Kenya (the name of the *CPK* from 1995)
BCP	Book of Common Prayer (1662)
CPK	Church of the Province of Kenya
ICET	International Consultation on English Texts
KAYO	Kenyan Anglican Youth Organization
KSHC	Kenyan Service of Holy Communion
NCCK	National Council of Churches in Kenya
PBTE	Provincial Board of Theological Education
SACTD	St Andrew's College of Theology and Development

ACKNOWLEDGEMENTS:

We are very grateful to Dr David M. Gitari for writing the Preface, to Joyce Karuri, Provincial Editor of the Liturgical Commission of the ACK, for her encouragement in the writing of this study, and to Uzima Press, Nairobi, for permission to reproduce extracts from *A Kenyan Service of Holy Communion* and *Modern Services*. The full texts are available from Uzima Press, PO Box 48127, Nairobi, Kenya.

First Impression September 2001

ISSN 0951-2667

ISBN 1 85174 477 0

Preface

by Dr David M Gitari, Archbishop of the Anglican Church of Kenya

Recent Liturgical Creativity in Kenya

The recent progress of liturgical creativity in the ACK has been very encouraging. For a very long time the Church had continued to depend on translated liturgies and songs which originated in the west from centuries ago. While this was acceptable formerly when the Church was still a mission church, over time there developed a need for liturgical revision. In 1975 the CPK authorized a modern *translation* of the Prayer Book services of Holy Communion, Baptism, Morning and Evening Prayer called *Modern English Services.*

Further commitment towards liturgical renewal was evidenced in 1987 when the Provincial Board of Theological Education (PBTE) embarked on serious liturgical work whose first fruits were seen in the publication of the *Kenyan Service of Holy Communion* in 1989. Among the scholars involved in this rigorous work was the late Rev John Nyesi who died shortly after the book was published. He will be remembered for a long time to come because of the third Post-Communion Prayer which he wrote: a very moving piece which one commentator termed as a 'prayer of a dying man'. As I wrote in the Preface on page 7 below (when Chairman of PBTE): 'This is not a modern translation or even an adaptation of the old, nor an importation of liturgical revision from the west but rather a new liturgy . . .' 'It is also universally appealing, an important ingredient of liturgical credibility.

This book has been in use now for over ten years and has flavoured the celebrations of the Lord's Supper not just within the perimeters of the ACK but also elsewhere in the Anglican Communion. The service was used during the opening service of the Lambeth Conference at Canterbury Cathedral in 1998. One liturgical scholar in a review wrote: 'This pioneering by Kenya is in principle a model for the whole Anglican Communion . . . the rite is a market leader'.

Two years after the publication of the *Service of Holy Communion*, a follow-up book of *Modern Services* was published in 1991, comprising the services of Morning Prayer, Evening Prayer, Baptism, Admission to Communion, Confirmation and Commissioning, the latter two services being only intended for study in dioceses pending permission for authoritative use by the Province. This book has now been in use for close to ten years and has become very popular in the cathedrals and colleges and several urban churches. Like the Holy Communion book, its use is limited mainly to urban populations because of language. There has been an attempt to embark on vernacular translations but this will only become a dynamic process when the whole prayer book has been published in English.

After the publication of *Modern Services*, PBTE met a number of times to study and recommend the remaining draft services for publishing. Some of these are not very frequent, but are vitally important. They are: Making of Deacons, Ordination of Priests, Consecration of Bishops, Dedication of Churches, Licensing of Lay Readers; Wedding Service; Blessing of Marriage; Burial; Reconciliation of a Penitent—among others. Many more services have been drafted and reviewed in a liturgical workshop. We hope to publish a complete new Kenyan Prayer Book at the end of 2001 or early in 2002.

The Synod of the ACK resolved towards the close of the millennium that, as a way of celebrating the new millennium, the publication of a new prayer book and a new hymnbook would take top priority. Our aim is to transform worship in the ACK through liturgical and musical renewal. So far, as well as the liturgical work that is in progress, there is also an active music commission which is writing, and putting together a rich collection of songs from around the country (and adjacent regions). The aim is to make a new indigenous sacred hymnbook (in Swahili) that would go alongside the Prayer Book. This project was preceded by similar initiatives in individual dioceses, more specifically in Kirinyaga diocese where the publication of *Nyimbo Cia Gucanjamura Ngoro* (Songs to Warm Our Hearts in Praise), has greatly changed the Church's musical lifestyle in worship. The hymnbook has also become acceptable in other Kikuyu-speaking churches.

In our liturgical and musical efforts we are attempting to publish works that enhance congregational participation and bring about the much desired satisfaction that good worship facilitates. Probably this is best summarized in the words of *The Kanamai Statement* that the 'liturgy needs to be open to opportunities for the expression of joy and suffering, of death and hope, affirming people's deepest affections'.[1] We have happily seen this goal being achieved through some of the services that have already been put to use, for instance in the *Service of Holy Communion* and *Modern Services*, and the more indigenous form of sacred music that has lately been introduced in worship. I am delighted to say that the beauty of our liturgical initiatives is not only being felt at home but also far abroad. I have received numerous requests from scholars, publishers and church leaders for permission to use certain liturgical excerpts from our services. We recognize and appreciate the commitment and charisma of all who participated in the Kenyan liturgical initiatives and to Canon Graham Kings in particular who, apart from his rich liturgical poetry, also worked hard on the manuscripts to ensure that features of outstanding Kenyan inculturation were an integral part of the services.

I am very grateful to Graham Kings and Geoff Morgan for writing this scholarly study of the recent Kenyan Liturgies and to the Alcuin/GROW Joint Board for publishing it. This in effect gives our efforts a higher international profile and is therefore a challenge and an encouragement to us to complete our liturgical mission, which began about 14 years ago. In his concluding remarks regarding the liturgical work in progress, Geoff Morgan quoted from the report of ACC-7's *Many Gifts, One Spirit*: 'The influence of the Old Prayer Book is waning, though a recognizably Anglican worshipping character persists. Yet this needs to be consciously sustained, expressed, renewed, and re-expressed'.

I return to my words in the Preface on page 7 below that creative work is 'the first fruits of liturgical renewal' and 'an exciting foretaste'.

The Most Rev Dr David M Gitari
Archbishop of the ACK & Bishop of Nairobi, March 2001

1 D Gitari (ed) *Anglican Liturgical Inculturation in Africa : The Kanamai Statment 'African Culture and Anglican Liturgy'*, (Alcuin/GROW Liturgical Study 28, Nottingham, England, 1994), p 40.

Introduction

by Geoff Morgan

The fact that the *Kenyan Service of Holy Communion (1989) (KSHC)* was chosen and used for the opening eucharist of the 1998 Lambeth Conference of Anglican bishops shows clearly the growing African influence on the shaping of Anglican theology and liturgy. Already at Lambeth 1988 the weight of African and Kenyan arguments were felt globally. Dr. David Gitari, the present Primate of the ACK, chaired the Resolutions Committee and played a leading role in the passing of Resolutions 22 (Christ and Culture), and 43 (Evangelism and Mission). In particular, Gitari promoted the notion of gospel as the judge of culture.[2] The choice of the Kenyan Communion Service also showed the wish of the bishops in particular to recognize the contribution of African and Kenyan practice towards the uniqueness of the overall structure of Anglican liturgical theology.

What then is distinctive about Anglican liturgy? What specifically would make an Anglican believer feel at home walking into a church service in an unfamiliar part of the world? Given there were no language barrier, this would depend on some recognition of a common shape in the worship, no matter how diverse the cultural expression of the common faith might be. How could a Kenyan Anglican believer be comfortable attending a service in a parish of the Church of England or of the Episcopal Church of the United States? Or an American or British Anglican attending a service in a parish in the Anglican Church of Kenya? Before Independence in 1963, the *Book of Common Prayer (BCP)* alone shaped much Anglican worship in Kenya. Worldwide liturgical renewal has led to cross-currents of influence[3] which have had a strong bearing on Kenyan Anglicanism amongst others, and now prayers from Kenya are being used in Anglican churches in other continents[4].

In this study we take the view that Kenyan Anglican ecclesiology has encouraged the indigenous expression of faith in post-Independence Kenya—with its 42 main ethnic groups—and that, contrary to what one might think, this has brought freedom, and not captivity. Liturgy—that holy space where forms of words, movement, crafts, music, silences between words and sacramental actions are woven together—is increasingly a culturally liberating instrument. It has been used both as a tool, excavating and restoring religious traditions, and as a symbolic weapon in social and political events. You will notice certain features if you enter the new library and chapel of SACTD, Kabare, in Kirinyaga diocese. Firstly you will see an evocative wood-carving of Christ on the cross on the main door (see front cover), and another carving of the Last Supper can be seen on the chapel

2 *Op.cit* p 6.

3 e.g. John Carden, *Morning, Noon and Night, Prayers and Meditations from the Third World*, (Church Missionary Society, London, 1976); Desmond Tutu, *An African Prayer Book*, (Hodder & Stoughton, London, Sydney, Auckland, 1995).

4 The new Anglican Kenyan services have been used in whole or in part in a number of places in the UK including York, Salisbury and Chelmsford Cathedrals, training colleges and mission agency conferences.

door upstairs. A text in brass stands over the entrance to the Archive Department:

> Look to the rock from which you were cut and to the quarry from which you were hewn.
>
> *Isaiah 51.1 (NIV)*

African oral culture and memory have much to teach the Western church. By way of parallel, in the introduction to an anthology, the Irish poet, Seamus Heaney explains the process of gathering poems 'on traditional bardic lines' as 'a memory bank, a compendium of examples'.[5] In Western churches the number of books needing to be given out before a church service can be embarrassing. However, in the liturgical 'singing schools' in Kenyan Anglican churches, confirmands can be required to learn and recite the catechesis from the *BCP*, albeit in a second or third language, and schoolchildren compose and perform their own scriptural hymns *a cappella*. Liturgy serves therefore to jog the memory and Africa in particular teaches us not to forget. Through the eucharistic *anamnesis*, we reach back to the beginning of time itself, to the 'Lamb slain from the foundation of the world' (Rev. 13.8). As a European searching for Christian origins in an African context, this present researcher has felt closer to the divine source of the gospel, and it is instructive to see the part which Kenyan liturgy has to play in this. However, liturgy also has a distinctive role in both affirming and challenging a traditional past, and in joining up the vast religious and political history (including Western missionary influence) with what the future will bring for Kenya in terms of unity and stability in multi-cultural and vernacular diversity.

There are certain features in the ACK which make it distinctively Anglican, and there is gain in seeing family likenesses across cultures. The international exchange of Anglican liturgies not only assists Western churches to learn about mission from African ones, for example, but also provides the means to compare processes of liturgical renewal and Anglican identity within diverse cultures. This brings with it great hopes for the future of liturgy and mission in the Anglican Communion.

Part 1 contains texts, historical background and commentary. It includes most of the main text from *A Kenyan Service of Holy Communion* (1989), some extracts from *Modern Services* (1991), and from an Environmental Litany (1991). These selections were chosen, and the background and commentary were written, by Graham Kings.[6]

Part 2 focuses on the sociological, anthropological and theological context of the liturgical renewal which is taking place in the ACK. This was written by Geoff Morgan, who drew on his MPhil dissertation on this topic.[7]

5 S Heaney and T Hughes (eds), *The School Bag*, (Faber and Faber, London, 1997) xvii.

6 In 1987-1991 Kings served as editorial secretary of the liturgical commission of the CPK, while he was Director of Studies and Vice-Principal of St Andrew's Institute, Kabare, 1985-1991.

7 In 1989 and 1996 Morgan made research visits to Kenya which were written up as: 'An Analytical, Critical and Comparative Study of Anglican Mission in the Dioceses of Nakuru and Mount Kenya East, Kenya, from 1975' (Short title: 'Anglican Mission and Liturgy in Kenya'), MPhil (Open University/Oxford Centre for Mission Studies, 1997).

PART ONE: LITURGICAL TEXTS AND COMMENTARY
(Graham Kings)

1
A Kenyan Service of Holy Communion, 1989

A. THE TEXT[8]

Preface

The Church of the Province of Kenya was founded on two books: the Bible and the Prayer Book. For many years we have had modern English translations of the Bible and in 1975 the Church authorized a modern translation of the services of Holy Communion, Baptism, Morning and Evening Prayer.

Now we have a new liturgy of Holy Communion. This is not a modem translation or even adaptation of the old, nor an importation of liturgical revision from the West, but rather a new liturgy which has grown out of recent developments in African Christian Theology and liturgical research. It is both thoroughly Biblical and authentically African, both faithful to Anglican tradition and refreshingly creative.

The draft was prepared in 1987 and after two years of experimental cathedral and college use, the Provincial Synod gave approval for its revision at a consultation of the Provincial Board of Theological Education in 1989, and publication. A Kiswahili translation is being prepared and vernacular translations are also planned.

These are the first fruits of liturgical renewal in the Church of the Province of Kenya and an exciting foretaste of the future new Prayer Book. As we use this service, and are fed by his holy Word and holy Sacrament, let us enjoy worshipping the God of our fathers, through Jesus Christ his Son in the power of the Holy Spirit.

The Rt Revd David Gitari
Bishop of Mount Kenya East
Chairman of the Liturgical Commission of the CPK, Advent 1989

The Preparation

1. *At the entry of the ministers the people stand. A hymn may be sung. The minister presiding welcomes the people with these or other appropriate words:*

2. *Minister* The Lord be with you.
People **And also with you.**

A Scripture sentence is read by the Minister [pages 2 and 3]

3. *Minister* The earth is the Lord's and all that is in it
People **Let the heavens rejoice and the earth be glad.**
Minister Our help is in the name of the Lord:
People **Who made heaven and earth.**
Minister I was glad when they said to me:
People **'Let us go to the house of the Lord.'**
Minister Praise the Lord:
People **The name of the Lord be praised.**

8 Due to the constraints on space the whole text (with notes, sentences, seasonal variations, and full rubrics) is not included and where the text is available elsewhere (e.g. ASB Collect for purity and ICET Gloria and Nicene Creed) these are only given a heading and a note in square brackets.

4. *Minister* Let us pray.
The people kneel. One of the following prayers for purity is said by all the people.

either
All **Almighty God,**
you bring to light things hidden in darkness,
and know the shadows of our hearts:
cleanse and renew us by your Spirit,
that we may walk in the light
and glorify your name,
through Jesus Christ, the Light of the world. Amen.

or [ASB Collect for Purity]

5. [6. and 7.] ***The Commandments***
[Ten Commandments, or Ten Commandments with the New Testament Interpretation, or the Summary of the Law]

The Gloria

8. *Either version of the Gloria may be sung or said.*
Minister We stand to glorify the Lord.

The people stand. The first version of the Gloria may be accompanied by regular clapping.

Minister Glory to the Father,
People **Glory to the Son,**
Minister Glory to the Spirit,
People **For ever Three in One.**
Minister Be glorified at home,
People **Be glorified in church,**
Minister Be glorified in Kenya,
People **Be glorified in Africa,**
Minister Be glorified on earth,
People **Be glorified in heaven.**
Minister Glory to the Father,
People **Glory to the Son,**
Minister Glory to the Spirit,
People **For ever Three in One.**
Minister Hallelujah,
People **Amen.**

9. [The second version of the Gloria is the ICET text]

10. *During Lent Only*
[The petitions 'Lord have mercy']

11. *The Prayer for the Day*

Ministry of the Word

12. *Old Testament Reading*

13. *The Epistle*

14. *A hymn, anthem or psalm may be sung or read.*

15. *The Gospel*

16. *A hymn may be sung.*

17. *The Sermon*

18. *The Creed introduced with the words:*

Minister We stand together with Christians throughout the centuries, and throughout the world today, to affirm our faith in the words of the Nicene Creed.
[ICET 1975 text, amended to read 'for us and for our salvation...']

The Intercessions

Instead of, or in addition to, the following litany of intercession, other words may be used, prayerful songs may be sung between intercessions, or people may be encouraged to join in open prayer. The leading of the intercessions may be shared among the people. The Intercessions may be introduced as follows:

Minister Let us pray.
The people kneel.

Either This Litany

19. *Leader* May the bishops and leaders of our churches have wisdom and speak with one voice.
People **Amen. Lord have mercy.**
Leader May the leaders of our country rule with righteousness.
People **Amen. Lord have mercy.**
Leader May justice be our shield and defender.
People **Amen. Lord have mercy.**
Leader May the country have peace and the people be blessed.
People **Amen. Lord have mercy.**
Leader May the flocks and the herds prosper and the fish abound in our lakes.
People **Amen. Lord have mercy.**
Leader May the fields be fertile and the harvest plentiful.
People **Amen. Lord have mercy.**

Leader May we and our enemies turn towards peace.
People **Amen. Lord have mercy.**
Leader May the love of the Father touch the lonely, the bereaved and the suffering.
People **Amen. Lord have mercy.**
Leader May the path of the world be swept of all dangers.
People **Hallelujah. The Lord of Mercy is with us.**

or Prayers of Intercession

20. *Leader* Let us pray for the Church.
Almighty God, our heavenly Father bless and guide all our bishops, pastors, church workers and all your faithful people. Grant wisdom to our archbishop . . . and to our bishop . . . that under them we may be led in the unity of your Holy Spirit. May all who confess your holy name continue to witness by serving their neighbours, loving their enemies and working together for the extension of your kingdom in and beyond our land.
Graciously hear our prayer:
People **We beseech you O Lord.**
Leader Let us pray for our nation.
Merciful Father, protect and guide our President . . . and all who are in authority under him that we may be governed in the way of peace, love and unity. May our leaders exercise your authority without fear or favour so that justice may roll down like waters and righteousness like an everflowing stream.
Graciously hear our prayer.
People **We beseech you O Lord.**
Leader Let us pray for the needs of the world.
Loving Father, your Son grew in wisdom and stature, in favour with God and man: as he brought your good news to the poor, we now bring to you those who are suffering from hunger, poverty and sickness, and who are under oppression and exploitation. Your kingdom come, your will be done, in transforming their lives and in inspiring us to share your gospel, so that friends and strangers may be saved.
Graciously hear our prayer.
People **We beseech you O Lord.**
Leader Let us thank God for the lives of those who have departed in Christ.
Gracious Father, we heartily thank you for our faithful ancestors and all who have passed through death to the new life of joy in our heavenly home. We pray that, surrounded by so great a cloud of witnesses, we may walk in their footsteps and be fully united with them in your everlasting kingdom.
Grant the prayers of your family, Father.
People **Through Jesus Christ, our mediator.**

The Prayers of Penitence

The people remain kneeling.

21. *Minister* Hear the words of challenge and comfort our Saviour Christ says to all who follow him:
If anyone would come after me, let him deny himself, take up his cross and follow me. For whoever would save his life will lose it; and whoever loses his life for my sake will save it. (*Luke 9.23-4*)
Come to me all of you who are tired of carrying your heavy loads, and I will give you rest. (*Matthew 11.28*)
So, all of you who repent of your sins, who love your neighbours and intend to lead a new life, following the way of Jesus, come with faith and take this holy sacrament to strengthen you.
Let us reverently confess our sins to Almighty God.

22. *All* **Almighty God, Creator of all,**
you marvellously made us in your image;
but we have corrupted ourselves
and damaged your likeness,
by rejecting your love and hurting our neighbours.
We have done wrong and neglected to do right.
We are sincerely sorry and heartily repent of our sins.
Cleanse us and forgive us by the sacrifice of your Son;
Remake us and lead us by your Spirit, the Comforter.
We ask this through Jesus Christ our Lord. Amen.

23. *Minister* Almighty God,
whose steadfast love is as great
as the heavens are high above the earth:
remove your sins from you,
as far as the east is from the west;
strengthen your life in his kingdom,
and keep you upright to the last day;
through Jesus Christ our merciful High Priest. **Amen.**

24. *All* **Thank you, Father, for forgiveness.**
We come to your table as your children,
not presuming but assured,
not trusting ourselves but your Word.
We hunger and thirst for righteousness,
and ask for our hearts to be satisfied
with the body and blood of your Son,
Jesus Christ the Righteous. Amen.

The Ministry of the Sacrament

25. ***The Sharing of the Peace***

The people stand.

Minister The peace of the Lord be always with you.
People **And also with you.**
Minister Let us offer one another a sign of peace,

The people greet each other with a handshake or other appropriate gesture.

26. *As the Holy Table is prepared for communion, bread and wine may be brought to the minister by the people or by his assistant. A hymn may be sung, during which the offering is collected. If there is no collection the minister moves directly to section 27.*

Minister All things come from you O Lord,
People **And of your own have we given you.**

The Prayer of Thanksgiving

The people remain standing.

27. *Minister* We remain standing for thanksgiving and remembrance.
Is the Father with us?
People **He is.**
Minister Is Christ among us?
People **He is.**
Minister Is the Spirit here?
People **He is.**
Minister This is our God.
People **Father, Son and Holy Spirit.**
Minister We are his people.
People **We are redeemed.**
Minister Lift up your hearts.
People **We lift them to the Lord.**
Minister Let us give thanks to the Lord our God.
People **It is right to give him thanks and praise.**
Minister It is right and our delight to give you thanks and praise,
great Father, living God, supreme over the world,
Creator, Provider, Saviour and Giver.
From a wandering nomad you created your family;
for a burdened people you raised up a leader;
for a confused nation you chose a king;
for a rebellious crowd you sent your prophets.
In these last days you have sent us your Son,
your perfect image,
bringing your kingdom, revealing your will,
dying, rising, reigning, remaking your people for yourself.
Through him you have poured out your Holy Spirit,
filling us with light and life.

Special Thanksgivings shall be said at this point when appropriate (sections 39—47).

Therefore with angels and archangels,
faithful ancestors and all in heaven,
we proclaim your great and glorious name,
forever praising you and saying:

People **Holy, holy, holy Lord . . . Hosanna in the highest.**

The presiding minister performs the traditional actions of taking the bread and breaking it etc. either during the words of institution, or at Section 30. The people remain standing.

Minister Almighty God, Owner of all things,
We thank you for giving up your only Son to die on the cross,
for us who owe you everything.
Pour your refreshing Spirit on us
as we remember him in the way he commanded,
through these gifts of your creation.
On the same night that he was betrayed
he took bread and gave you thanks;
he broke it and gave it to his disciples, saying:
'Take, eat; this is my body which is given for you;
Do this in remembrance of me.'

People **Amen. His body was broken for us.**

Minister In the same way, after supper he took the cup
and gave you thanks; he gave it to them, saying:
'Drink this, all of you; this is my blood of the new covenant
which is shed for you and for many for the forgiveness of sins.
Do this as often as you drink it, in remembrance of me.'

People **Christ has died,**
Christ is risen,
Christ will come again.

Minister We are brothers and sisters through his blood.

People **We have died together,**
we will rise together,
we will live together.

Minister Therefore, heavenly Father,
hear us as we celebrate this covenant with joy,
and await the coming of our Brother, Jesus Christ.
He died in our place, making a full atonement
for the sins of the whole world,
the perfect sacrifice, once and for all.
You accepted his offering by raising him from death,
and granting him great honour at your right hand on high.

People **Amen. Jesus is Lord.**

Minister This is the feast of victory.

People **The Lamb who was slain has begun his reign. Hallelujah.**

The Communion

28. *Minister* As Jesus taught us, so we pray: [The Lord's Prayer]

29. *Minister* Christ is alive for ever:
People **We are because he is.**
Minister We are one body:
People **We share one bread.**
Minister We break this bread:
People **To remember his death.**
Minister We share this cup:
People **To receive his life.**
Minister Draw near with faith:
People **Christ is the host and we are his guests.**

The presiding minister and his assistants receive the bread and wine. Then he holds the bread, and one of his assistants holds the wine, and they declare to the people:

30. *Minister* The body of our Lord Jesus Christ which was given for you, keep your body and soul in eternal life. Take and eat this in remembrance that Christ died for you, and feed on him in your hearts, by faith, with thanksgiving.
Assistant The blood of our Lord Jesus Christ, which was shed for you, keep your body and soul in eternal life. Drink this, in remembrance that Christ's blood was shed for you and be thankful.

31. [Distribution]

After Communion

The people stand. One of the following prayers is said.

32. *All*
Almighty God, eternal Father,
we have sat at your feet,
learnt from your word,
and eaten from your table.
We give you thanks and praise
for accepting us into your family.
Send us out with your blessing,
to live and to witness for you
in the power of your Spirit,
through Jesus Christ, the First Born from the dead. Amen.

or

33. *All* [A second post communion prayer] *or*

34. *All*
O God of our ancestors, God of our people,
before whose face the human generations pass away;
We thank you that in you we are kept safe for ever,
and that the broken fragments of our history

are gathered up in the redeeming act of your dear Son
remembered in this holy sacrament of bread and wine.
Help us to walk daily in the Communion of Saints,
declaring our faith in the forgiveness of sins
and the resurrection of the body.
Now send us out in the power of your Holy Spirit
to live and work for your praise and glory. Amen.

The Blessing

35. *One of the following blessings may be used.*

The people accompany their first three responses with a sweep of the arm towards the cross behind the Holy Table, and their final responses with a sweep towards heaven.

Minister All our problems,
People **We send to the cross of Christ.**
Minister All our difficulties,
People **We send to the cross of Christ.**
Minister All the devil's works,
People **We send to the cross of Christ.**
Minister All our hopes,
People **We set on the risen Christ.**
Minister Christ the Sun of Righteousness shine upon you
and scatter the darkness from before your path:
and the blessing of God almighty,
Father, Son and Holy Spirit,
be among you, and remain with you, always.
People **Amen.**

or

36. ['The peace of God which passes all understanding…']

The Dismissal

37. *One of the following may be used*
['Go in peace to love and serve the Lord…']

or

Minister Go out into the world, rejoicing in the power of the Spirit.
People **Thanks be to God.**

38. *A final hymn may be sung as the ministers depart.*

B. A KSHC: HISTORICAL BACKGROUND

In October 1986 the PBTE of the Church of the Province of Kenya (CPK), chaired by David Gitari, recommended the writing of a Kenyan Service of Holy Communion. Gitari has been the inspiration and driving force for encouraging liturgical renewal in Kenya since becoming Bishop of Mount Kenya East in 1975.[9] The 1662 Book of Common Prayer had been used in English, in Kiswahili (the general trade language of East Africa) and in vernacular translations (e.g. Kikuyu) for many years. As mentioned in the preface, a modern translation of the Prayer Book services of Holy Communion, Baptism and Morning and Evening Prayer, was published in 1975,[10] but what was desired was a new liturgy, which would reflect and rejoice in traditional and modern aspects of Kenyan culture.

In early 1987 a member of the CPK Liturgical Commission produced a draft service of Holy Communion which was circulated to the CPK theological colleges and cathedrals for experiment and comment. Gideon Ireri, Principal of St Andrew's Institute for Theology and Development, Kabare[11] and also secretary of the diocesan Liturgical Commission, was about to go on a year's study leave to Yale Divinity School. He asked the college worship committee (the present author and eight students) to respond to the draft.

The eight-page critique suggested that the draft was mostly a copy of the ASB 1980 liturgy, and that it could have been written in England.[12] Various suggestions were also made.[13] The Liturgical Commission asked Ireri and the Institute to revise the draft. Instead, a completely new draft liturgy was written at Kabare by the worship committee in June 1987 and soon caused considerable interest.[14]

In February 1988 a Provincial 'Partners in Mission' Consultation took place at Kabare. This involved several consultants from other provinces of the Anglican Communion who discussed the five-year priorities which had been set by the CPK. Their enthusiastic response to the draft liturgy led to its wider circulation as copies were taken to England and to other provinces of the Anglican Communion. In the same year, Phillip Tovey provided some of the draft text, particularly the Prayer of Thanksgiving and the blessing, and commented on it in his book *Inculturation: the Eucharist in Africa*.[15]

9 For Gitari's background and theological influence see Graham Kings 'Proverbial, Intrinsic and Dynamic Authorities: A Case Study on Scripture and Mission in the Dioceses of Mount Kenya East and Kirinyaga' in John Stott et al. *The Anglican Communion and Scripture* (Regnum Books, Oxford, 1996) pp 134-143, republished and expanded in *Missiology* 24 (1996), pp 493-501. For further historical background see John Karanja, *Founding an African Faith: Kikuyu Anglican Christianity, 1900-1945* (Uzima Press, Nairobi, 1999), which is the publication of his Cambridge PhD thesis, 1993.

10 Church of the Province of Kenya, *Modern English Services* (Uzima Press, Nairobi, 1975). Christopher Carey, CMS missionary in Nairobi, oversaw this modern translation.

11 The Institute was founded at Kabare, in the southern foothills of Mount Kenya, in 1978 by Gitari. Kabare was a pioneer site for the first preaching of the gospel in the region of Kirinyaga, in 1910. The Institute has since been renamed 'St Andrew's College of Theology and Development' (SACTD). Ireri is currently Bishop of Mbeere.

12 Elimu Njau, a Kenyan artist, has commented in another context: 'Don't copy. Copying puts God to sleep.' (Source untraced).

13 The archive of SACTD, holds a copy of this manuscript and copies of the drafts of the liturgy.

14 'This liturgy seems to me to break new ground for Africa and even to blaze a trail which the rest of the continent might enthusiastically follow and even develop, feeling a shade rueful that they had not thought of it first. I mean among Anglicans, of course; these forms are merely a tentative excursion into what the Independent Churches have been doing for two generations – and their worship is a key factor in their phenomenal growth.' Roger Bowen, 'The Revised Kenyan Service of Holy Communion' *News of Liturgy* No. 154 (Oct 1987), pp 2-3.

15 Tovey, Phillip, *Inculturation: the Eucharist in Africa* (Alcuin/GROW Liturgical Study 7, Grove Books, Nottingham, 1988), pp 38-39.

The draft was scrutinized by the Provincial Commission, which moved the Gloria from its place after the communion to 'the preparation' and added a fine post-communion prayer, specially written by John Nyesi, a former Principal of St Paul's United Theological College, Limuru. The new liturgy was circulated for experiment and comment to the colleges and cathedrals.

In April 1989 the Provincial Board of Theological Education, again chaired by David Gitari, met at Mombasa to consider the liturgy. Very few revisions were made[16] and *A Kenyan Service of Holy Communion* was published by Uzima Press, in Advent 1989.[17] In 1990 it was reviewed in *News of Liturgy*,[18] and in the bulletin of the Evangelical Fellowship in the Anglican Communion, by Colin Buchanan,[19] made available outside Kenya through Grove Books and David Gitari wrote an article in the *Church Times* entitled 'An Offering from Africa to Anglicanism'.[20] At the end of May and the beginning of June 1993, Gitari hosted an international consultation on African Culture and Anglican Liturgy at Kanamai, near Mombasa.[21] In the 1990s the rite was used in various English theological colleges, cathedrals and mission conferences.[22] Its wider use, outside of Kenya, culminated in the opening eucharist of the 1998 Lambeth Conference in Canterbury Cathedral.

C. A KSHC: COMMENTARY ON PARTICULAR PARAGRAPHS

1. 'The minister presiding'. In Kenya it is inappropriate to use the word 'President' to refer to anyone other than the Head of State. Therefore this phrase was used, which in most of the rest of the text is shortened to 'Minister'.

2. Sentences. Some of these are common to other rites. The unusual ones here are: 'God rained down upon them manna to eat, and gave them the grain of heaven.'(Psalm 78.24); 'You shall have a song as in the night when a holy feast is kept; and gladness of heart, as when one sets out to the sound of the pipe to go to the mountain of the Lord, to the Rock of Israel.' (Isaiah 30.29); and 'Why spend

16 See the comments below.

17 The CPK publishing house.

18 Colin Buchanan, 'A Kenyan Service of Holy Communion' in *News of Liturgy* No. 182 (Feb 1990), p 7.

19 'This rite is a market-leader. It takes seriously both the liturgical tradition and the needs of its own Province. It drives in the inculturation wedge, and prises apart the set-in-concrete style of liturgical colonialism (self-inflicted by the colonized as that sometimes is)...This pioneering by Kenya is in principle a model for the whole Communion.' Colin Buchanan, 'A Kenyan Service of Holy Communion' in *Evangelical Fellowship in the Anglican Communion Bulletin* No. ? 1990, p 18.

20 David Gitari, in *Church Times* 6 April 1990. 'We believe this new rite is both thoroughly biblical and authentically African, both faithful to Anglican tradition and contextually creative.'

21 Council of Anglican Provinces in Africa, *African Culture and Anglican Liturgy: the report of the Kanamai Consultation 1993* (Grove Books Ltd, Nottingham, 1993). See D. Holeton (ed.), *Liturgical Inculturation in the Anglican Communion* (Alcuin/GROW Joint Liturgical Study no 15, Nottingham, 1990).

22 In particular St John's College, Nottingham, Ridley Hall and Westcott House, Cambridge, Chelmsford Cathedral and York Minister, CMS conferences at Selly Oak, the Gospel and our Culture conference at Swanwick (1992). Peter Hancock, in a letter to *News of Liturgy*, compared the Kenyan rite to the newly published Church of England draft eucharistic rite: 'The English responsive liturgy was worthy, well-meaning, and had some merit; but it sounded as though it had been put together by a committee (perhaps it had). The Kenyan rite, on the other hand, though a bit "tribal" in some respects, had enormous vitality, and with a few emendations...could be used by an English congregation... It seemed that the English rite lacked soul – or do I mean poetry?' *News of Liturgy* No. 167 (Nov 1988), pp 6-7. See also Ian Tarrant, 'Anglican Liturgical Reform in Congo/Zaire: the Story, Comparisons and Reflections'. (St George's Windsor, unpublished paper, 1999).

money and get what is not bread, why give the price of your labour and go unsatisfied? Listen to me and you will have good food to eat.' (Isaiah 55.2).

3. Opening Responses from Psalms 24.1; 124.8; 122.1; and 135.1.

4. New Collect for Purity. The theme of light stems from the Johannine literature in the New Testament and the East African Revival concept of 'walking in the light' with someone, which involves being honest with them even when it may hurt.

6. New Testament Interpretation of the Law. This quotes from 1 Timothy 5.8 concerning honouring parents and from Ephesians 4.28 concerning stealing.

8. Gloria. It starts at home and ends in heaven. The regular three-beat clap, suggested in the rubric, is often used in political and fund-raising events to praise local politicians: here is it redirected towards the Holy Trinity. The clap is on the syllables *Glo...to...Fath...* and *glor...fied...home...*etc. It also works well without the regular clapping. It was originally written for the consecration of Embu cathedral (in the diocese of Mount Kenya East) and in that service these were the first words David Gitari pronounced immediately after he entered his new cathedral.

18. Creed. The new words of introduction stress the catholicity of the Church in time and space. In the phrase '...for us and for our salvation . . . ' the word 'men' was omitted to provide 'invisible inclusiveness.'

19. Litany. This is based on an ancient Kikuyu litany and at certain points it has been Christianized and adapted. Jomo Kenyatta, the first President of Kenya, recorded the original in his book *Facing Mount Kenya*,[23] which runs:

> Say ye, the elders may have wisdom and speak with one voice.
> **Praise ye Ngai.[24] Peace be with us.**
> Say ye, that the country may have tranquillity and the people may continue to increase.
> **Praise ye Ngai. Peace be with us.**
> Say ye, that the people and the flocks and the herds prosper and be free from illness.
> **Praise ye Ngai. Peace be with us.**
> Say ye, the fields bear much fruit and the land may continue to be fertile.
> **Praise ye Ngai. Peace be with us.**

In this rite, the line 'May justice be our shield and defender' is part of the Kenyan national anthem[25]; the prayer that the 'people may continue to increase' was changed to 'and the people be blessed' since Kenya had one of the highest population explosions in the world;[26] 'fish' have been added to 'flocks and herds'

23 Jomo Kenyatta, *Facing Mount Kenya* (Heinemann, London, 1938), p 130.

24 *Ngai* is the ancient Kikuyu name for God, which is also used in the Kikuyu Bible and the translation of the Book of Common Prayer, thus manifesting the theme of continuity between *Ngai* and the God and Father of our Lord Jesus Christ. See Graham Kings, 'Facing Mount Kenya: Reflections on African Traditional Religion and the Bible'in *Anvil*, 4 (1987), pp 127-143.

25 This addition was specifically requested by Gitari, who quoted the phrase in many sermons on justice. See David Gitari, *Let the Bishop Speak* (Uzima Press, Nairobi, 1989) and David Gitari, *In Season and Out of Season: Sermons to a Nation* (Regnum Press, Oxford,1996).

26 This adapted prayer may amount to the same thing, since to 'be blessed' is often taken to mean '...with children' who are indeed a blessing from the Lord.

for they are very important at the coast and in western Kenya and aspects of the lives of various ethnic groups needed to be included;[27] the petition 'may we and our enemies turn toward peace' was added because Jesus' radical call to love our enemies is counter-cultural to all cultures in the world, including the various cultures in Kenya; the petition about 'the lonely, the bereaved and the suffering' etc was added at Gitari's request; the final petition reflects the naturally winding paths in the Kenyan countryside.

20. Prayers of Intercession. The fourfold shape follows the ASB but the prayers are all new.

(a) **Prayer for the Church:** this includes again a petition about 'loving our enemies' as well as 'neighbours' (Luke 10. 29-37) and echoes Kenyatta's Kiswahili slogan of 'Harambee' ('let us all pull together') in the phrase 'working together for the extension of your kingdom...'

(b) **Prayer for the Nation:** this echoes President Moi's 'Nyayo' ('footsteps' philosophy').[28] When he was asked what 'Nyayo' meant he expounded the slogan as standing for Peace, Love and Unity. In this prayer the petition for 'justice' is added to these three well-known words, using the phrase from Amos 5.24 'let justice roll down like waters...'. In 1981 Gitari edited a book expounding biblically the three words 'peace, love and unity' and added an extra chapter on the missing word 'justice'.[29]

(c) **Prayer for the Needs of the World:** this links the model of Jesus' growth (Luke 2.52) with the needs of the world and reflects the Lord's prayer ('your kingdom come, you will be done...') and an holistic theology of mission ('in transforming their lives and in inspiring us to share your gospel'). Luke 2.52 was a key verse for Gitari's theology of mission and development strategy. He believed that every child in the diocese should have the chance of developing as the child Jesus did in mind, body, spirit and society. Jesus grew in:

Wisdom	(mind)	which implies educational involvement
Stature	(body)	which implies community health work
Favour with God	(spirit)	which implies evangelism
Favour with people	(society)	which implies social justice.

(d) **Thanks for those Departed in Christ:** this mentions 'ancestors' who are vitally important in African life. Not all ancestors are implied but those

27 The Kikuyu ethnic group led the moves for education and colonial independence and dominated the political process under Kenyatta's regime.

28 Originally Moi implied that this meant he was following in the footsteps of Kenyatta, but the opposition to Moi soon maintained that it really meant 'you all have to follow in my footsteps'. See G. Patrick Benson, 'Ideological Politics Versus Biblical Hermeneutics: Kenya's Protestant Churches and the Nyayo State' in Holger Bernt Hansen and Michael Twaddle (eds), *Religion and Politics in East Africa* (James Currey, London, 1995), pp 177-199. Benson served on the staff of St Andrew's Institute, Kabare, from 1979-1987 and was Gitari's Communication Secretary from 1988-90.

29 National Council of Churches of Kenya, *A Christian View of Politics in Kenya: Love, Peace and Unity* (NCCK, Nairobi, 1983). Gitari was in fact the editor, although not mentioned on the title page.

who were 'faithful' to the Supreme God, before the arrival of the gospel, as well as the early converts. There is also an echo of Hebrews 12.1 'surrounded by a cloud of witnesses...' and the 'Nyayo' slogan: but here it involves following the 'footsteps' of the saints.

21. Introduction to Confession. Jesus' challenging warning about the cost of discipleship (Luke 9.23-24) has been added to the BCP (and ASB) 'comfortable word' (Matthew 11.28). This contributes a balance of 'challenge and comfort' and avoids any implications of 'cheap grace'.[30]

22. Confession. This combines the positive view of human beings created in the image of God (Genesis 1.27), with strong language of 'corruption', 'damage', 'rejecting' and 'hurting', which echoes Jesus' summary of the law (love of God and of our neighbour). There is alliteration (three 'm's) in 'marvellously made us in your image' and assonance in the contrast of 'image' and 'damage.' The prayer has a trinitarian ending.

23. Absolution. This is based on Psalm 103.11-12: 'For as the heavens are high above the earth, so great is his steadfast love toward those who fear him; as far as the east in from the west, so far does he remove our transgressions from us'. There is also prayer for present strengthening (the penitent is *already* in the kingdom of God) and ultimate keeping (when the kingdom fully comes on the last day). The phrase 'keep you upright' is a positive version of Jude 24 ('keep you from falling').

24. Thanksgiving for Forgiveness. This prayer is a transformation of Cranmer's 'Prayer of Humble Access' and placed in a radical new setting. In the BCP it interrupted the eucharistic prayer; in the ASB it was appended to the intercessions[31] and in Common Worship it is relegated to an appendix (and often omitted). The context here, in the Kenyan service, provides a liturgical response to absolution, which is often missing in other rites. It picks up Cranmer's reference 'gathering up the crumbs under your table' to the gentile Syrophoenician woman (Mark 7.28) 'even the dogs under the table eat the children's crumbs,' and makes it more positive. In Kenya, an implicit comparison of a human being with an animal is a profound insult: 'dog collars' are renamed 'clerical collars'. So the implicit link with the 'dogs under the table' has been transformed into the radical gospel privilege of being the children of God eating at his table.[32] 'Not presuming' (echoing Cranmer) is coupled with an evangelical doctrine of assurance, 'but assured'. This crucial difference is elucidated by the contrasting foundations 'not trusting ourselves, but your Word'.[33]

The prayer continues with the link between 'hunger' and 'righteousness', quoting the Sermon on the Mount (Matthew 5.6) and 1 John 2.1 'Jesus Christ the Righteous' (which Cranmer used as part of the 'comfortable words'). The word 'satisfied' is regularly used in English in Kenya for the translation of the Kiswahili 'Umeshiba?' ('have you have sufficient food?'). Here it is coupled with the word

30 For the concept of 'cheap grace' which offers the comfort of religion without the radical challenge of discipleship, see Dietrich Bonhoeffer, *The Cost of Discipleship* (SCM press, London, 1964).

31 The ASB also had an excellent new alternative prayer in the appendix. This was written by David Frost, who also wrote the ASB post-communion prayer 'Father of all...'

32 This is picked up again in the paragraph 32, the first post communion prayer.

33 There is assonance between 'assured' and 'Word'.

'hearts' taken from Cranmer's invitation to communion: 'feed on him in your hearts, by faith with thanksgiving.' This emphasizes that we feed on Christ not in our mouths (some object to the over-realistic language in modern versions for 'the prayer of humble access') but in our hearts.

27. The Prayer of Thanksgiving. It is unusual to begin a eucharistic prayer with a series of rhetorical questions. The English development 'The Lord is here' is transformed into trinitarian questions, which combine to form a sort of catechetical, credal and responsive introduction to the prayer. They are usually spoken with vigour and elicit loud declarations of faith in God being present. Having focused on God, the affirmations turn to the identity of the congregation and in the language of the covenant ('we are his people', 'we are redeemed'). The traditional 'sursum corda' follows.

The phrase 'right and our delight' echoes, with assonance, concepts of 'duty and joy'. The list of seven titles of God reflects African ways of praying, which often accumulate adjectives. It includes Jesus' typical address to God ('Father'), and the summary Old Testament title ('Living God').[34] In the original draft the word 'Provider' was 'Allocator' which tried to translate the Kikuyu words for God 'Ngai' or 'Mugai.'

The root of these words implies 'divide' i.e. Ngai judiciously divides out the heritage of the land, some to one ethnic group or clan and some to another.[35] The word 'Allocator' sounded odd and did not convey this subtlety so it was changed to 'Provider,' which links well with 'Creator', but loses the hint of judging.

The next paragraph tightly packed and runs through biblical theology from Abraham to Pentecost. The first sentence focuses on the Old Testament (which is too often omitted at this point, but is particularly emphasized in African Christian theology). It has cumulative phrases beginning 'From . . . for . . . for . . . for'. The developing contrasts between family . . . people . . . nation . . . crowd,' have matching adjectives and verbs 'created . . . raised up . . . chose . . . sent . . .'. In this sentence Old Testament and contemporary Kenyan resonances are combined. 'From a wandering nomad . . .' echoes the deuteronomic covenantal creed concerning Abraham ('A wandering Aramean was my father . . .' Deut 26.5-10) and the present large numbers of nomads in northern Kenya; 'For a burdened people you raised up a leader . . .' echoes Moses (Exodus 3) and also Jomo Kenyatta;[36] 'the king' echoes David's line (2 Samuel 7) and presidents of Kenya; 'the rebellious crowd' and 'prophets' refers to the condition of Israel before the exile (Isaiah and Jeremiah) and to Kenyan current political life (with the challenges of Gitari, Muge and others).

34 See David Gitari and G. Patrick Benson (eds), *The Living God*, (Uzima Press, Nairobi, 1987) and Graham Kings, 'God the Father in the New Testament' on pp 55-76.

35 A similar use of the concept may be found in the question posed to Jesus in Luke 12.13: '"Teacher, bid my brother divide the inheritance with me." But [Jesus] said to him, "Man, who made me a judge or divider over you?"'

36 For Kenyatta's appropriation of biblical material see John Lonsdale, 'Wealth, Poverty and Civic Virtue in Kikuyu Political Thought' in Bruce Berman and John Lonsdale (eds), *Unhappy Valley: Conflict in Kenya and Africa. Book Two: Violence and Ethnicity* (James Currey, London, 1992), pp 315-504. See also a forthcoming biography of Kenyatta by Lonsdale.

The move to the New Testament in the second sentence is eased with reference to Jesus' parable of the vineyard (Mark 12.1-11) where 'servants' are sent and then finally the 'son' and to Hebrews 1.1 ('. . . God spoke to our fathers by the prophets; but in these last days he has spoken to us by a Son . . .'). The description of Jesus as the 'perfect image' continues the Hebrews theme with Hebrew 1.3 ('He reflects the glory of God and bears the very stamp of his nature...') as well as linking with the confession ('marvellously made up in your Image'). 'Bringing your kingdom, revealing your will' echoes the Lord's prayer[37] and leads into four cumulative participles which sum up Good Friday, Easter Day, Ascension and Pentecost: 'dying, rising, reigning, remaking your people for yourself . . .'

The introduction to the Sanctus again mentions faithful ancestors in heaven[38] and the Sanctus itself does not continue into a Benedictus (for the presence of Christ has been emphasized in the opening questions). The breaking of the bread is either done during the narrative of institution (as in the BCP) or at paragraph 29.

The next sentence has the sound 'o' repeated three times (in an echo of the Sanctus). '*Own*er of all things[39], we thank you for giving up your *on*ly Son to die on the cross, for us who *owe* you everything.' The phrase 'giving up' is used deliberately (rather than a suggested amendment 'giving us') to resonate with Romans 8.32 'He did not spare his own Son, but gave him up for us all...' which itself is a direct contrast to the story of Abraham and Isaac in Genesis 22 where Isaac was, after all, spared.[40] The epiclesis is a short prayer for the Holy Spirit to be poured on the people (not the elements), which uses the same word ('pour') as earlier used about Pentecost.[41]

With the phrase 'We are brothers and sisters through his blood' we come to the hidden heart of the prayer. In many African ethnic groups there is a traditional concept of 'blood brotherhood', whereby friends bind themselves together, in a sort of covenant, through rubbing blood together from slight cuts in the arm. This concept here resonates with the new covenant through the blood of Christ and includes women. The phrase has a double meaning: through the blood of Christ, we are brothers and sisters with him and also with each other. This is underlined with the following responsive echoes of Romans 6.4-11: 'We have died together, we will rise together, we will live together'.[42] The repeated word

37 It also echoes Matthew 6.33 'Seek first the kingdom of God and his righteousness.'

38 See below on paragraph 34.

39 Another African title for God.

40 Jürgen Moltmann, has called this 'one of the most unheard-of phrases in the New Testament', *The Crucified God: the Cross of Christ as the Foundation and Criticism of Christian Theology* (ET, SCM Press, London, 1974), p 191. 'We must understand "deliver up" in its full sense and not water it down to mean "send" or "give"...A theology of the cross cannot be expressed more radically than it is here.' *ibid.* p 191.

41 See Acts 2.18 (quoting Joel 2.29) '...I will pour our my Spirit...', Romans 5.5 '...God's love has been poured into our hearts through the Holy Spirit...' and Acts 3.19 '...that times of refreshing may come from the presence of the Lord.' See also David Kennedy, 'The Epiclesis in the Eucharistic Rites of the Church of England and the Churches of the Anglican Communion: with special reference to the period 1900-1994' (PhD thesis, Birmingham, 1996), p 466.

42 Paul here uses several Greek verbs with the prefix 'syn' ('buried with', 'united with', 'crucified with' 'die with', 'live with') to emphasize the community link with Christ and with each other. This echo of Roman 6 also brings baptismal theology into the heart of the eucharist.

'together' has a powerfully binding effect on the congregation.[43]

The eucharistic prayer leads onwards to the climax with 'awaiting the coming of our Brother, Jesus Christ'. This Christological concept of Christ as our 'Elder Brother' has been much developed in African Christian theology. The elder brother, in an African family, is particularly someone to look up to and to follow. New Testament references to Jesus as our brother include Matthew 25.40 ('. . . to these the least of my brothers you do also to me'), John 20.17 ('. . . go to my brothers and say to them'), Romans 8.17 ('. . . fellow-heirs with Christ') and Hebrews 2.11 ('. . . he is not ashamed to call them brothers').[44]

There are further echoes of Cranmer's words in 'He died in our place, making a full atonement for the sins of the whole world, the perfect sacrifice, once and for all.'[45] Then the resurrection and ascension are related specifically to the Father's accepting of the offering of the Son. The climax comes with the congregational 'Amen', the ancient short creed of 1 Corinthians 12.3, 'Jesus is Lord', and the songs of Revelation (Rev 5.9-10, and 19.6-8), which also resonate with Jesus' parables of the messianic feast. Having begun with Abraham in Genesis the eucharistic prayer ends with the Lamb in Revelation.

29. Responses during the Fraction and Invitation. The original draft ran:

Minister I am because we are.

People **We are because he is.**

This reflected John Mbiti's distinction between western individualism and African corporate identity. Mbiti, a Kenyan Anglican, who at that time was working in Switzerland, is a father of African Christian theology. He contrasted Déscartes' 'I think therefore I am' with the African concept of 'I am because we are, and since we are therefore I am.'[46] The draft took this further and extended it to refer to our dependence on Christ's life: we exist because Christ is alive. In the revision process this was rightly considered too esoteric and it was changed to pick up the last phrase of the previous Lord's prayer '...now and for ever.'

Minister Christ is alive for ever

People **We are because he is.**[47]

The pun in 'Christ is the *host* and we are his guests' is deliberate and, according to ecclesiastical tradition, may be taken or left.

33. First Post-Communion Prayer. The image here is of children outside an elder's hut. This was more obvious in the original draft, which had 'Great Elder' instead

43 It was said that this phrase was particularly poignant at the opening eucharist of Lambeth 1998, for the night before the bishops had heard stories of their fellow bishops undergoing persecution.

44 During the revision process, there was some opposition to calling Jesus our brother: 'it brings him down to our level'. Another Kenyan theologian pointed out that this was the whole purpose of the incarnation. The original concluding response to the intercessions was '...through Jesus Christ our Elder Brother' and this was revised to '...through Jesus Christ, our Mediator.' However, the reference to '...the coming of our Brother, Jesus Christ' was kept in the eucharistic prayer.

45 For an excellent study of patristic eucharistic sacrifice see Joseph Galgalo, 'Eucharistic Sacrifice: a Theological Study of the Sacrificial Interpretation of the Early Eucharist and its Role in the Economy of Salvation (circa 30-202 AD),' (PhD thesis, Cambridge, 2001). Galgalo, a student at St Andrew's College, Kabare 1990-1993, now lectures at St Paul's United Theological College, Limuru, Kenya.

46 See John S. Mbiti, *African Religions and Philosophy* (Heinemann, Nairobi, 1969).

47 This means both 'we exist because he exists' and 'we will live for ever, because he lives for ever.'

of 'Eternal Father.' However, there was opposition to this name for God (which comes from the Meru ethnic group) since it was not found in the Bible. There are echoes of Acts 22.3 (Paul sat at the feet of the elder Gamaliel) and Col 1.18 ('first born from the dead').

34. Third Post-Communion Prayer. This was added at the revision stage and the original was written by John Nyesi, former Principal of St Paul's United Theological College, Limuru, and a Luo from Western Kenya. He was a brilliant theologian, very ill at the time, and he died in 1988. At the Provincial liturgical conference someone who did not know who wrote this prayer commented: 'this is a prayer of a dying man.' The address to God as 'God of our Ancestors' sets the tone for the whole prayer, it resonates with 'the God of Abraham, Isaac and Jacob'. We are transient here, but God is eternal and keeps us safe in his eternity. There are echoes of the feeding of the five thousand ('fragments being gathered') which itself is a foretaste of the last supper.[48] There are also echoes of the Nicene creed ('Communion of Saints, forgiveness of sins and resurrection of the body'). Kwame Bediako, a leading Ghanaian theologian, has quoted Nyesi's whole prayer, together with other references to ancestors in this service (intercession and Sanctus):

> 'Here, past and present meet, the ancestors are fully within the new community of faith, and the living and the "living dead" pray together, indicating what one possible response to the question of ancestors could well be in the meeting of the Christian religion and the African world.'[49]

35. The Blessing. This is based on an ancient litany of the nomadic Turkana ethnic group, from the north of Kenya. Its foundation as a curse on their enemies has been transformed into a blessing. Traditionally the Turkana, with a dramatic sweep of their arms to the west, would send all their problems, difficulties and works of evil to the Karamajong, a nomadic ethnic group in what is now Uganda. When a group of Turkana, who had migrated southwards became Christians their Kenyan evangelist stressed Jesus' call to love our enemies and suggested that instead of sending those things to the Karamajong they should send them to the setting sun. They agreed.[50] In the first draft,[51] the blessing ran:

Minister All our problems,
People **we send to the setting sun;**
Minister All our difficulties,
People **we send to the setting sun;**

48 The 'four fold action' of 'taking', 'blessing', 'breaking' and 'distributing' are in both.

49 Kwame Bediako, *Christianity in Africa: the Renewal of a Non-Western Religion* (Edinburgh University Press, Edinburgh, 1995), pp 229-230. It is in his section entitled 'Towards a Theology of Ancestors'.

50 On 23 July 1991 the present author interviewed Paulo Lobur, the Turkana elder at Alamach, near Isiolo, Kenya, through a translator, Peter Ekai. Lobur was the elder who traditionally led this christianized litany, and often talked in rhythmic style. He said: 'People have to stand for these prayers. Only the eldest person present may lead it.' He later prayed for Ekai and the present author including: 'Apa, you help me because you are the only source. Forgive me because I have not made any idol to resemble you. Give blessings to these men, all the time, night and day. Send away evil spirits to go far from them. The vehicle they are traveling in – may it be safe. All people are yours. Because you are everywhere, help those on journeys, wherever they are. These two brothers who are still learning – help them and strengthen their sight for what is needed. Bless their families.'

51 See Tovey, *Inculturation*, 1988.

Minister All the devil's works,
People **we send to the setting sun;**
Minister All our hopes,
People **we set on the risen sun.**[52]
Minister Christ the Sun of Righteousness shine upon you ...[53]

During the Provincial Liturgical Conference theologians from the dioceses in the west of Kenya complained 'Well, no wonder we are having problems: you are sending them all to us.' A revision was called for. Since it began as a curse, curses in the New Testament were considered. In Galatians 3.13 Paul writing about the cross, stated that 'Christ has redeemed us from the curse of the law, having become a curse for us...'. Therefore the revised blessing replaced the phrase 'to the setting sun' with 'to the cross of Christ' and the phrase 'on the risen sun' with 'on the risen Christ'. This has proved to be a very powerful end to the service as the people three times sweep their arms towards the cross, the only place in heaven and on earth which can cope with all our problems, difficulties and the devil's works. The physical sensation of movement, and the whole congregation joining in with it, are finally very moving.

2

Modern Services, 1991: Background, Extracts and Commentary

(a) Historical Background

From 29 April to 2 May 1991 the PBTE conference at St Andrew's Institute, Kabare[54] considered five newly drafted services: 'Morning and Evening Prayer' and 'Admission to Holy Communion' written at Kabare; 'Baptism' at St Mark's College at Kapsabet, in Western Kenya (Stephen Kewasis, Bishop of Eldoret and Mark Ashcroft, Principal of the college, were particularly involved) and 'Confirmation and Commissioning' written by David Gitari, Bishop of Kirinyaga. Jephthah Gathaka (Kirinyaga Communications Secretary) presented a well-argued case for the admission of children to Holy Communion before Confirmation. The services were only slightly revised.

At the Provincial Standing Committee of Synod in July 1991, Bishop Gitari presented a further theological background paper on the new initiation services, especially concerning admission of children to Holy Communion before Confirmation. He stressed that sacramental initiation is complete in baptism and argued that the new service of Confirmation and Commissioning:

(a) *removed* the theological impressions from earlier services that the candidates were now being made full members of the Body of Christ, that they were receiving the Holy Spirit for the first time and that they were being granted admission to Holy Communion;

52 A contrasting pun on the word 'set'.
53 Malachi 4.2 (ASB blessing for Advent).
54 There were about 70 delegates from nearly all of the 14 dioceses of the CPK.

(b) *kept* the theological point that the candidates were confirming their baptismal vows;

(c) *added* the theological stress that they were being commissioned for the service and witness of the Church in the world.[55]

The PBTE recommended concerning the initiation services that:

(a) adults should have two services: 'Baptism' (including admission to Holy Communion) by the local Priest, and 'Confirmation and Commissioning' by the Bishop.

(b) children should have three services: 'Baptism' in infancy by the local Priest (on the repentance and faith of their parents and godparents), 'Admission to Holy Communion' by the Priest at about the age of 6 or 7 (after a period of instruction on the meaning of the sacraments) and 'Confirmation and Commissioning' by the Bishop at the age of completing primary education (11,12 or 13) after a period of instruction on faith, service and witness.

The Synod at that time authorized the services of 'Morning Prayer', 'Evening Prayer' and 'Baptism' for experimental use and the services of 'Admission to Holy Communion' and of 'Confirmation and Commissioning' for study only, but the latter was authorized in February 2001. The booklet was published in August 1991.

(b) Morning Prayer: Extracts and Commentary[56]

1. Introduction and Welcome

Leader We have come together, the people of God,
drawn by his Spirit, longing for his word,
to praise the holy name of the Lord
to share his glorious news of grace,
to pray for our needs and the pain of the world,
to rejoice in his love and be sent in his peace.

Leader We are heirs of the Father,
People **joint heirs with the Son**
Leader renewed in the Spirit,
People **together we are one**.

These opening responses echo the foundational verses concerning the family of God in Romans 8.15-17: 'For you did not receive the spirit of slavery to fall back into fear, but you have received the spirit of sonship. When we cry "Abba! Father!" it is the Spirit himself bearing witness with our spirit that we are children of God, and if children then heirs, heirs of God and fellow heirs with Christ . . .'

2. Sentences. The selection includes both traditional ones (e.g. Luke 15.18) and new suggestions (e.g. 'Whom have I in heaven but you? And there is nothing on

55 David Gitari, 'A Theological Background Paper to the New Initiation Services Especially Concerning Admission to Holy Communion Before Confirmation' (unpublished paper for the Provincial Standing Committee of Synod of the CPK, July/August, 1991), p 4.

56 CPK, *Modern Services: Morning Prayer, Evening Prayer, Baptism, Admission to Holy Communion, Confirmation and Commissioning* (Uzima Press, Nairobi, 1991). The full text is not given here, due to constraints of space, and so particular extracts are followed immediately by comments on them.

earth that I desire besides you' (Psalm 73.25) 'Come, let us go up to the mountain of the Lord that he may teach us his ways and that we may walk in his paths' (Is 2.3).

3. Confession.

Eternal Father, God of our ancestors,
before your power all things tremble,
but through your Son, we approach your throne.
We have done wrong and neglected to do right;
our sins weigh heavily on our hearts;
Lord have mercy, count them not against us.
Grant us the joy of forgiveness
and lighten our hearts with the glory of Christ,
who died and rose again for us. Amen.

The first line balances the New Testament emphasis on the fatherhood of God with the theme of the third post-communion prayer in the Communion service, 'God of our ancestors', thus emphasizing the continuity of the concept of God in African Traditional Religion and the God and Father of our Lord Jesus Christ. The second line echoes the Prayer of Manasseh verse 4 (in the Apocrypha) 'before your power all things quake and tremble' (REB, 1989) and is balanced by the echo from Hebrews 4.16 'let us with confidence draw near to the throne of grace . . .' The heart of the confession is a play on the Hebrew word for 'glory' (kabod) which originally designated 'weight', 'substance' or what could be called 'gravitas' and developed, according to George Caird, under the influence of Ezekiel, into 'brightness' or 'radiance'.[57] Therefore sins 'weigh heavily . . .' and there is a plea: 'lighten our hearts with the glory of Christ'. 'Lighten' covers the meanings of 'make less heavy' and also of 'brighten'. 'Glory' carries the meanings of 'weight' and of 'radiance'. The irony of praying for our hearts 'to be made less heavy by something which is heavy' is probably missed by most people, but was deliberate. The themes of 'heart' and 'lighten' also echo Matthew 11.29-30: 'Take my yoke upon you, and learn from me; for I am gentle and lowly in heart, and you will find rest for your souls. For my yoke is easy, and my burden is light.'

4. Absolution.

The God and Father of our Lord Jesus Christ
rejoices at repentance and declares his acceptance.
The dead are alive, the lost are found.
His goodness and mercy will follow you
all the days of your life,
and you will live in the house of the Lord for ever. Amen.

The joy of the Father, and the clear declaration of forgiveness, in the first part of this prayer is based on the parable of the prodigal son in Luke 15.11-32, especially verse 24 'for this my son was dead, and is alive again; he was lost, and is found.' The second half of the prayer, in its assurance, echoes Psalm 23.6.

57 See G. B. Caird, *The Language and Imagery of the Bible* (Duckworth, London, 1980), p 76.

6. Gloria.

Leader Glory to the Father in whom all things began,
People **Glory to the Son who became the Son of Man,**
Glory to the Spirit who inspires and renews
The Lord our God for ever! Alleluia!

This new Gloria is used also after the psalm and canticles.

7. Alternative Gloria.

Leader The glorious Son of God on high
People **is born for us through Mary's womb:**
Leader the homeless Prince of Peace on earth
People **is crushed and lies in Joseph's tomb:**
Leader the reigning Lord of Life and death
People **breaks the bonds of time and doom.**

This alternative, responsive Gloria may be sung, the rubrics say, between Christmas and Epiphany and between Easter and Pentecost. It is based on the song of the angels in Luke 2.14 'Glory to God in the highest, and on earth peace among people with whom he is pleased' and covers the incarnation, cross and resurrection with three titles of Christ.

8. First Canticle. The choice is a version of the Jubilate (Psalm 100.3), or the ASB version of the Venite (without the final verses) or the Song of Habakkuk (Habakkuk 3.17-18). The latter is adapted to Kenya: 'Though the mango tree does not blossom . . . the crop of the coconut fails...'

9. Second Canticle (after the Old Testament Lesson). The choice is a new canticle 'The Song of the Messiah', the Benedictus or the Song of Paul (Colossians 1.15-18).

The Song of the Messiah

Jesus the Seed of Abraham
blesses the nations:
Jesus the Prophet like Moses
frees the oppressed:
Jesus the Lord of King David
leads his people:
Jesus the Servant of the Lord
suffers and saves:
Jesus the Son of Man
destroyed and raised.

This new song draws on five of the messianic titles in the Law and the Prophets, which are highlighted in the New Testament. See Genesis 12.3, Deuteronomy 18.15f., 2 Samuel 7.12f., Isaiah 53.4, and Daniel 7.13-22.

The 'Song of Paul' in Colossians 1 is transposed from the third person singular ('He is the image of the invisible God . . .') to the second person ('You are the image of the invisible God . . . By you, O Christ, were all things created . . . You are before everything'). The effect is startling and turns narrative into praise.

10. Third Canticle (after the New Testament Lesson). The choice is the Song of Jesus, the Te Deum or the Song of Revelation (combining Revelation 19.6-8; 4.11; 5. 9-10; 15.3-4 and 5.13). The Song of Jesus is based on the work of Joachim Jeremias, the scholar of Aramaic, who discovered a particular way of speaking preferred by Jesus. He translated many of Jesus' words in the Greek New Testament back into his mother tongue of Aramaic and found that many of the most memorable phrases had a particular rhythm or beat.[58]

The Song of Jesus

Love your enemies,
do good to those who hate you,
bless those who curse you,
pray for those who abuse you.
I was hungry and you gave me food,
thirsty and you gave me drink,
a stranger and you welcomed me,
naked and you clothed me,
sick and you visited me,
in prison and you came to me.
The blind receive their sight,
the lame walk, the lepers are cleansed.
The deaf hear, the dead are raised:
the good news is preached to the poor
and blessed are those not offended at me.

These are taken from Luke 6.27, Matt 25.35-36, Luke 7.22-23 and Luke 10.21 and combined together, for they all have the same rhythm in Aramaic, which can also be felt in English. Reciting the words of Jesus the Poet has been found to be very moving. The words of David, Zechariah, Mary and Simeon have been sung for centuries in Anglican and other liturgies: why not the words of Jesus himself?

21. Versicles and Responses

The last four of these are:

Leader In the valley of the shadow of death;
People **protect us with your rod and staff.**
Leader Like trees planted by the waterside;
People **grant us the fruit of your Spirit.**
Leader Send us out as the salt of the earth;
People **and as the light of the world.**
Leader May the earth be filled with your glory;
People **as the waters cover the sea.**

They echo Psalm 23.4, Psalm 1.3 and Galatians 5.22, Matthew 5.13-14, and Habakkuk 2.14 and pick up the themes of light, water and salt.

58 See Joachim Jeremias, *New Testament Theology Volume 1* (SCM Press, London, 1971) pp 21-29 in the section 'Ways of Speaking Preferred by Jesus'.

24. Prayer for Grace

Almighty God,
you have been our Guard through the night,
keep us in your care through the day;
walking in your light, bearing witness to your way,
seeking first your kingdom and seeing you in everyone;
guide us in the footsteps of your Son,
and lead us on the path to your everlasting Day;
through Jesus Christ our Lord. Amen.

This picks up the themes of God keeping his people in Psalm 121.5-8 and Philippians 4.7, the East African revival emphasis on 'walking in the light' and on 'bearing witness,'[59] echoes of Matthew 6.33 and Matthew 25.34-46, the themes of 'footsteps'[60] and the Day of the Lord.

34. Prayer for Rain

Almighty God, Giver of life and strength,
Creator of rain and sky, dust and earth,
Preserver of people and plants and animals:
as our cattle leave their enclosures,
as we work on a dry and weary land
we look to you, our living God;
pour on us your heavenly showers,
quench our thirst, strengthen our herds,
raise our crops and refresh our land;
through Jesus Christ, the water of life. Amen.

After three titles of God, both pastoralists (e.g. the Masai) and farmers (e.g. the Kikuyu) are included, there is an echo of Psalm 63.1 and there are five cumulative bold petitions 'pour . . . quench . . . strengthen . . . raise . . . refresh . . .' for rain.

35. Prayer after Silence.

Your silence is full, irresistible;
your presence is joy unspeakable.
people drifting into mind
we lift to you and pray they find
  health in sickness,
  life in deadness,
  strength in weakness,
  light in darkness.
their loss you bear mysteriously;
your peace you share eternally.

This has proved to be a very popular prayer after a period of silent intercession. It is based around Psalm 16.11 'In your presence there is fullness of joy . . .'.

59 See the comments on the new collect for purity in the service of Holy Communion.
60 See the comments on President Moi's slogan of 'Nyayo' ('footsteps') in the Prayer for the Nation in the service of Holy Communion.

39. Alternative Forms of Blessing.

May the Lord of the harvest bless your crops:
your maize and beans,
your potatoes and rice,
your coffee and tea.
May the Lord of creation bless your animals:
your cows and bulls,
your sheep and goats,
your chickens and pigs.
May the Lord of all life bless your families:
your grandfathers and grandmothers,
your husbands and wives,
your sons and daughters.
The blessing of God almighty . . .

The rubric runs: *'A blessing which may vary according to the local crops and livestock and which may be said outside the church, with the minister stretching his hand towards the fields etc.'* It is based on a regular blessing by David Gitari.

(c) Evening Prayer: Extracts and Commentary

8. Canticles after the First Lesson. **The Song of Mary** or **The Song of Blessings** (Matthew 5.3-10). See the comments on page 29 above about the words of Jesus.

10. Canticles after the Second Lesson. **The Song of Simeon, the Song of the Kingdom** or **the Song of Christ's Mission.**

The Song of the Kingdom

Do not be anxious about your life;
what you shall eat,
what you shall drink,
or what you shall wear.
Look at the birds of the air;
they neither sow nor reap nor gather into barns
and yet your heavenly Father feeds them.
Consider the flowers of the field;
they neither toil nor spin,
yet Solomon in all his glory
was not clothed like one of these.
Seek first the kingdom of God
and his righteousness,
and all these things shall be yours as well.

This is taken from Matthew 6.25-33 and has the same rhythmic beat as the other songs of Jesus. The Song of Christ's Mission (Phil 2.5-11) is transposed into the second person singular (like the Song of Paul in Morning Prayer): 'You, O Christ, were in the form of God . . . You emptied yourself taking the form of a servant . . . and every tongue confess that you are Lord: to the glory of God the Father.'

21. Prayer for Protection.

O Lord our God,
how majestic is your name in all the earth.
created from the dust of the ground,
inspired with your Spirit, we live:
breathless at the end, we die,
and return to the dust of death.
Grant us your blessing this night
in the sure hope of rising with Christ
and rejoicing with him in your glory;
through him who is alive and reigns with you
and the Holy Spirit, one God world without end. Amen.

The first part is based around echoes of Psalm 8.1, Genesis 2.7, Psalm 104.29-30 and Psalm 22.15. The second part mixes the assurance of the resurrection with rising with the sun at the beginning of the next day.

(d) Baptism: Extracts and Commentary

17. The Prayer of Thanksgiving over the Water

Minister O give thanks to the Lord for he is good;
People **for his steadfast love endures for ever.**
Minister For the blessing of water;
People **we thank you, Lord.**
Minister For saving Noah and his family through the water of the flood;
People **we thank you, Lord.**
Minister For bringing the children of Israel safely through the Red Sea out of slavery in Egypt, to the freedom of the promised land;
People **we thank you, Lord.**
Minister For your Son, Jesus Christ, who was himself baptized in the river Jordan;
People **we thank you, Lord.**
Minister Hear our prayers as we obey your Son's command to go and baptize in the name of the Father, and of the Son and of the Holy Spirit;
People **hear us.**
Minister Sanctify this water for baptizing your servants;
People **sanctify.**
Minister Bless those who are to be baptized in it;
People **bless them.**
Minister May they be cleansed from all their sins;
People **be cleansed.**
Minister May they be united with Christ in this death and resurrection;
People **be united.**
Minister May they be born again by the Spirit to eternal life;
People **be born again.**

Minister May they be joined into the fellowship of the Body of Christ;
People **be joined.**
Minister Christ has defeated Satan and all evil powers!
People **Alleluia!**

This prayer, somewhat like the eucharistic prayer, builds up momentum as it is recited with its emphatic and short responses. It is based on the way of praying of the Pokot ethnic group from whom it came. The theology of baptism is rehearsed in the versicles and enforced in the responses.

20. **Ululations.** After the baptism the rubric states that *'ululations may be made'*. These 'trillings with the tongue' usually by women, are the traditional African greetings at birth, circumcision, marriage and death and they take on the meaning of the context, here of new birth and circumcision (Col. 2.11-12).[61]

21. **Anointing (Optional)** The rubric runs: *'The sponsors or parents shall anoint each candidate with oil on the forehead saying*:

We anoint you in the name of the Anointed One.
You belong to us, we all belong to Christ.'

Messiah (Hebrew) and Christ (Greek) mean 'Anointed One'. The fact that it is not the priest but the sponsors or parents who anoint is significant. Amongst the nomadic Pokot people of western Kenya (and many others), the community traditionally anoint with oil at birth, at rites of passage and at death.[62]

(d) Admission to Holy Communion: Extracts and Commentary

3. Examination of the Candidates

Minister What do you understand as the meaning of your Baptism?
Candidates **I was baptized into Christ and died to sin.**
I have been made clean by him and now live for him.
I share his Spirit and am a member of his Church.
Minister What do you understand as the meaning of Holy Communion?
Candidates **We remember that Christ died for us.**
As we receive the bread and wine,
we feed on his body and blood,
in our hearts by faith with thanksgiving.
Minister What is required of those who come to Holy Communion?
Candidates **They should make sure**
that they have truly turned from their sins
and live for Christ,
that they trust him alone for salvation
and love their neighbours.

61 The editor of the *Church Times* commented (4 October 1991): 'I thought of ululation as howling: . . . ; and it seemed to me the height of tact that what a lot of babies were going to do anyway should be pre-programmed in this way as a deliberate liturgical act. But I gather that the sound here intended is a joyful one.'

62 When someone, at the Provincial theological conference in April 1991, objected to anointing in this liturgy saying 'It is not part of our tradition' (i.e. it implies Catholic tendencies), he was answered by Kewasis, 'Church tradition or African tradition? Among my people anointing is vitally important.'

Note the moves from 'I' (for Baptism) to 'we' (for Holy Communion) to 'they' (for the requirements). After renewal of baptismal vows there is the admission.

6. **Admission to Holy Communion**

Minister We were all baptized by the one Spirit,
Candidates **into one body.**
Minister We who are many are one body,
Candidates **for we all share one bread.**
Minister I, and the communicants of this parish,
admit you to be a partaker of Holy Communion,
in the name of the Father, and of the Son,
and of the Holy Spirit.
All **Amen.**
Minister Let us welcome these our brother and sisters,
as fellow partakers with us of the Lord's Supper.
All **We welcome you to share with us in the Lord's Supper.**
Happy are those invited to the marriage feast of the Lamb.
Alleluia!

There are echoes here of 1 Corinthians 12.13, 1 Corinthians 10.17 and Revelation 19.9. It is not just the minister who admits to Holy Communion but the minister and the communicants of the parish.

(f) Confirmation and Commissioning: Extracts and Commentary

9. The Making of Promises

Bishop So that all may know your intention and resolve, what is your pledge?
Candidates **We, about to be commissioned**
for the mission of Christ and his Church,
pledge to keep and walk in God's commandments
all the days of our lives,
and to read the Bible and pray regularly.
We pledge to proclaim Christ,
in season and out of season,
to obey him and to live in the fellowship
of all true believers throughout the world.
We pledge to be active in church,
to give to the work of the church,
to help the needy, support the poor,
and to be good stewards of all that the Lord has given us.
We pledge to uphold truth and justice,
and to seek reconciliation among all people;
The Lord being our helper.

In this service as well as being confirmed in their faith the candidates are called to make a serious commitment to holistic mission. Here are expressed desires for daily discipleship, evangelism, commitment to the church, compassion for the poor, respect for the earth, and the search for justice and reconciliation.

3

Environmental Litany: Extracts and Commentary

On Sunday 19 May 1991, Rogation Day, Bishop Gitari led a service at Trinity Church, Mutuma, in the southern foothills of Mount Kenya, overlooking Kamuruana Hill. Some local political leaders had used their position unjustly to acquire this beautiful hill. In order to build their hotel, the poor people who lived on the hill were evicted and the trees were cut down.[63] In his sermon, Gitari expounded the story of Naboth's Vineyard in 1 Kings 21.[64] He had phoned St Andrew's College, Kabare, to ask the students to produce a litany for the environment. They had searched concordances for references to trees, fields, cedars etc. and dug deep into the background.

The litany, apart from the final section, was deliberately made up only of scriptural quotations.[65] Its first section was headed 'Celebration of Creation' and had verses from Psalm 24.1-2, Psalm 104.16-17, Psalm 24.3-4. The second section was headed 'Judgement on Those who Destroy the Environment' and contained verses from the book of Isaiah, Isaiah 5.20-21; 13.2, 3,14-15; 5.8-9; 10.1-2; 37.23-24; 37.29. The following were originally directed against Sennacherib:

Reader By your servants you have mocked the Lord,
and you have said, 'With many chariots
I have gone up the heights of the mountains,
to the far heights of Lebanon;
I felled its tallest cedars,
I came to its remotest height,
its densest forest.' (*Isaiah 37.24*)

Bishop Thus says the Lord,

Reader 'Because you have raged against me
and your arrogance has come to my ears,
I will put my hook in your nose
and my bit in your mouth,
and will turn you back on the way
by which you came.' (*Isaiah 37.29*)

The final section was headed 'Hope for Creation' and had verses from Job15.7-9; Psalm 96.12-13, Isaiah 14.5 and 8, and 55.12:

Reader The pine trees and the cedars of Lebanon exult over you and say,

People **'Now that you have been laid low,
no woodsman comes to cut us down.'** (*Isaiah 14.8*)

Bishop For you shall go out in joy,
and be led forth in peace;
and the mountains and the hills before you
shall break forth into singing,

People **and all the trees of the field
shall clap their hands.** (*Isaiah 55.12*)

The Scriptures thus were used with performative force.[66] They were not just a quarry for pertinent texts but were alive with resonances across the years and the lands. This litany was reused at an ecumenical service in Uhuru Park, Nairobi, on 26 March 1999 to pray for the threatened forests of Kenya and especially Karura.[67]

63 For further details see Kings, 'Proverbial, Intrinsic and Dynamic Authorities'.
64 See D Gitari, *In Season and Out of Season: Sermons to a Nation* (Regnum Press, Oxford, 1996), pp 102-110.
65 For the full text see *News of Liturgy* (August 1991), pp 8-10.
66 Soon after this service, the local politicians fell from power.
67 NCCK and the Roman Catholic Church in Kenya, 'The Environment and the Integrity of God's Creation: Procession and Prayers . . . on 26 March 1999.' (unpublished paper).

Geoff Morgan

1
'Top Down' and 'Grass Roots'

The Anglican Communion and Kenyan Liturgy as a 'Top-Down' Process

According to the theologian, Stephen Sykes, liturgy is a controlling factor in ecclesiology, that is, in the formation of the identity of the local church. Acts of hearing, singing or reading of Scripture in the liturgy in a 'hermeneutic largely of communal praise' are set in the context of the recitation of the creeds, collects, prayers, canticles and responses, and hymns. This compendium, according to Sykes, more than anything else defines the doctrine, authority and integrity of Anglicanism.[68] An anthology of texts rather than one central liturgical text to be adapted, as in the Roman Catholic Church, characterizes the Anglican Communion.[69] Furthermore, this attendance to a common structure rather than one common text is sustained by the sense of need to relate worship to African cultures.[70] Nonetheless, the need to be 'part of a bigger whole' and to aim at limiting cultural differentiations in favour of well-blended African liturgies with a sense of history, theology and culture has been stressed.[71] The uniting effect of the Eucharistic structure was also noted at Kanamai as follows:

1. gathering together
2. telling the Christian story with intercessory prayer
3. (sharing) the meal with thanksgiving
4. sending out

This is because it is important for people themselves to discover the structure of the Eucharistic Prayer, and to compose their own prayers within that framework, rather than translate from English language sources.[72] In 1995, the Fifth International Anglican Liturgical Consultation stated that in the future, Anglican unity will find its liturgical expression not so much in uniform texts as in a common approach to eucharistic celebration and a structure which will ensure a balance of word, prayer and sacrament, and which bears witness to the catholic calling of the Anglican communion.[73] Commonality with some degree of rigour

68 S Sykes, *The Integrity of Anglicanism*, (Mowbrays, Cambridge, 1978)
69 D Gitari (ed), *Anglican Liturgical Inculturation in Africa*, pp 37-38.
70 This reflects an original Anglican tradition: 'It is not necessary that Traditions and Ceremonies be in all places one and utterly like . . . they . . . may be changed according to the diversities of countries, times and men's manners . . . ' 'Article 34, Of the Traditions of the Church'.
71 D Gitari (ed), *Anglican Liturgical Inculturation in Africa*, p 39.
72 D Gitari (ed), *Anglican Liturgical Inculturation in Africa*, p 38.
73 David R. Holeton (ed), *Renewing the Anglican Eucharist, Findings of the Fifth International Anglican Consultation, Dublin, Eire, 1995*, (Grove Worship Series 135, Grove Books, Cambridge, 1996) p 4.

rather than rigid uniformity is the mother of new Anglican liturgical invention and one can cite here what has been taking place in the ACK in the last ten to fifteen years. One might object that uniformity is exactly what is apparent since these liturgies are written in the medium of the English language. However, English has become the language of education, government and politics in Kenya and is, with Kiswahili, one of the two main languages which are therefore used in churches. However, vernacular liturgies have developed as well as translations and many pieces written in English have a different linguistic background or are composed on the basis of that background. In the next section we examine the emergence of authentic texts rather than their superimposition by a hierarchy or élite.

Kenyan Social History and Local Worship Styles from the 'Grass Roots'

There follow three snapshots, of a Neo-Pentecostal service, and two Anglican services[74], which were experienced by this researcher in Nakuru and Kirinyaga dioceses respectively. We will examine what extent these services represent what is foreign or indigenous, the public or private spheres, and how far they are élitist, or, alternatively, to what extent they spring from the 'grass-roots' in their origin. We begin with a short background to two dioceses, which, although it is not comprehensive of the scope of Kenyan Anglicanism, serves to set these reviews in context.

Social and religious background to Nakuru and Kirinyaga Dioceses

Nakuru diocese is inhabited by 'Kalenjin'-speakers, (that is Nandi, Tugen and Kipsigis peoples), and the Maasai, the traditional owners of the Rift Valley Provinces before European land alienation took effect, as well as by the Luo, the Luhyia, the Kamba and the Kikuyu. Here few feel that they are at home, and the Kikuyu are not yet so dominant in this area, although their economic middle class have certainly made inroads in the area by the purchase of farms.[75] In Kirinyaga diocese on the other hand the Kikuyu are dominant. The Kikuyu are one of the largest single ethnic groups representing 26%[76] of the entire population of Kenya. After the Kikuyu (5,146,000) who occupy traditionally the central part of the country there are the western Luyia (3,475,000) and the eastern central Kamba (2,146,000). According to a Kikuyu myth, *Ngai* (the Divine Being) gave the whole land south of Mount Kenya to them, a perception which is still strong amongst the Kikuyu peoples and influenced their growth in property ownership after the era of colonialism or colonial district boundaries.

Kirinyaga diocese is more densely populated, cultivated and homogeneously Kikuyu than cosmopolitan Nakuru town which is generally heterogeneous in its make-up as a centre of migration. In large areas of Nakuru diocese, however, there are more homogeneous groups and pastoralist peoples where identity and

74 The second of these is found in the Appendix.
75 Gavin Kitching, *Class and Economic Change in Kenya*, (Yale UP, New Haven / London, 1980).
76 *Kenya Democratic and Health Survey* (Nairobi, 1993).

ethnicity are formed and reformed around the givenness of ritual fields. The Kikuyu are not dominant in Nakuru; however it is well known as a politically dynamic town, a fact which may be related to its volatile populations. Both Kirinyaga and Nakuru dioceses have large areas of thinly populated and desertified land and pastoralist peoples in the north.

Kikuyu traditionally relate to the transcendent often by the association of divinity with a mountain and through a complex social organisation; for the Maasai and other more pastoral groups, the complexity of social organization is subject to the environment and traditional worship depends on the ritual slaughtering of undefiled animals from prized stock. Contrasting views of the divinity, either as found in relation to a mountain or to the sun (for more northern Kenyan communities) do not detract from a common monotheistic belief which these communities share.

To these particular communities (amongst the many in Kenya) came the givenness of a new ritual field, the Anglican liturgy, catechesis and symbology inherited from the *Book of Common Prayer (BCP)*. It was translated, with the Bible, into various vernacular languages, and a more striking contrast could not be imagined between the uniform Christian worship based on the English Reformation and the multi-ethnic, socially-diverse and politically-charged communities which Kenya represented, and into which it was introduced. For various reasons the Anglican forms were particularly appropriate. In the next chapter we will examine evidence that this was and continues to be so.

2
Contemporary Snapshots and Analysis

Snapshot One

Account of a Neo-Pentecostal Service: Chrisco Fellowship Service: Nakuru Town, 29/2/96 [77]

1. The lunchtime service took place in a hired public meeting hall in the town centre. An arrangement of benches in rows faced the front of the hall, posters declaring that 'Jesus Christ is enthroned in this place', and notifying of revival meetings adorned the walls.

2. A worship ensemble consisting of singers, a keyboard player, bass and lead guitars and drums was set up in front of the benches. Before the service began many gathered in the worship space and bowed their heads in devotion. A lead singer with a roving microphone led the singing, which modulated into expository and 'rap'-style prayer, and prayer in tongues, each one praying on his or her own. The prayer was in English and called for revival, for the blessing of bishops and leaders, and was addressed to God, e.g. 'Wrap us in Your Spirit, Lord.' This continued for 5 minutes.

77 *Chrisco* was founded by someone named Harridas in the 1980s. It is an indigenous, interdenominational mission church, and many mid-week supporters at this meeting also went to other churches.

3. There was then a mass rendition of the English hymn, 'There is power in the blood . . . ' which lasted 2 minutes, followed by more mass intercessory prayer, singing with tongues, and prayers for the 'President, the Vice-President, for Provisional, Divisional, District Officers, Chiefs, and Sub-chiefs, and for the fear of the Lord to come upon them'.

4. The hymn, *Asante sana Yesus*, (translated from the English 'Thank you thank you Jesus') was sung in Kiswahili for about 5 minutes and then the congregation was encouraged 'to shout praises out loud to the Lord'. This lasted another 5 minutes. After another Anglo-American hymn, that is to say, one composed originally in English and then translated, the pastor welcomed the congregation and announced that the collection would be taken during the next hymn, which was also Anglo-American.

5. Another period of public prayer followed in which the visiting preacher- using bilingual English and Kiswahili- commanded every ear to hear and receive the word. There were prayers for those who had requested it, announcement of some 'words of knowledge', and prophetic utterances directed at some specific people or needs.

6. The sermon followed in which the preacher opened with the question: 'Why do some situations come upon us?' The emphases were eschatological, on the sanctification of the faithful, and the coming revival. The congregation was exhorted to wave if it understood what he was saying, for example:

> We are all on our way to the promised land . . . I used to sometimes take a long route home from school for fun and to parental disapproval; God took the children of Israel on a long route to Canaan because he wanted to spend time with them. When there is no problem we are full of hallelujah, but when problems come our testimony evaporates. The people came to the Red Sea, Egypt was behind them and there was no going back (nods from congregation); they complained, 'Is this what you call Deliverance?' Remember where, how, and when God visited you. You have your holy ground, your burning bush; there is hope for you when you pass through the waters, when in financial crisis, or hopeless. The other day I met a woman who had marriage problems, who had attempted suicide, and she accepted Jesus, praise God . . .

This sermon lasted 30 minutes and was to be continued the next day.

7. Most people left rapidly to get back to work. In personal conversation the pastor was concerned to stress that revival was already present in their group, and that 'we (Chrisco) are here to bring individuals to Jesus, not communities.'[78]

Account of a Service at St. Matthew's Ngiriambu, ACK Diocese of Kirinyaga, 18/2/96

The worship setting was the new church which was built in 1982 after a 'harambee'[79] in 1976; the first church was built in 1936, its founding father being Samuel Mukuba, who had first come there to preach in 1919, and is remembered by the elders.

78 Morgan, 'Anglican Mission', p 139.

79 *Harambees* are Kenyan communal fund-raising endeavours.

Snapshot Two

Account of Service of Morning Prayer from the Kikuyu Book of Common Prayer, 11.00am.

1. The service began with a procession of the choir and clergy from the vestry through the entrance of the church to the chancel, singing an English hymn

2. The service was led by two lay readers and a female student from St Andrew's College.

3. The Kikuyu order of service was followed to a large extent, and notable were the chanted Psalms (in Kikuyu).

4. Hymns were interspersed regularly in the order, with the new hymn book, *Nyimbo Cia Gucanjamura Ngoro*—('Songs to Warm our Hearts in Worship') being used for the most part. Two hymns were sung from this book, a large minority of the congregation having purchased their own copies.

5. A member gave her 'testimony' in the form of a singing solo; another original Kikuyu hymn was sung while members brought their gifts up to the plate in the aisle before the chancel; then a prayer of offering was said.

6. This was followed by the introductions interpreted into Kikuyu, notices and financial appeals. One of these concerned a sick child. One of the lay readers was the master of ceremonies. This lasted half an hour.

7. After the sermon from the visiting preacher (of about half an hour) there was another hymn and an invitation to give again to the plate in *harambee*-style support for the child's medical fees.

8. The recessional hymn was a Kikuyu version of 'Guide Me O Thou great Jehovah'.[80]

Comparative Analysis of a Neo-Pentecostal and an Anglican Service

1. *Setting.*

The first area for comparison is that of context. The Chrisco service took place in a hired hall whilst the Anglican church had a long worshipping history and served both as a 'school chapel' and as a parish church. The congregations were distinctive in that one was urban (Nakuru) and contained largely working or professional young people, and the other was rural (the *BCP* Service in Ngiriambu).

Symbolisms of authority or ecclesiology can be compared: the use of the microphone and electronic music, and a suit and tie worn by the preacher, as against processions and robes and a platform and pulpit in the Anglican church.

2. *Forms and language.*

The contrast between the forms of service was striking in that the Neo-Pentecostal liturgy was led orally by the worship-leader and intercessor, rather than from the text of the Kikuyu *BCP*. Whilst the Chrisco service appeared 'freer', it lasted strictly no more than 45 minutes, and was largely held in English. The *BCP* service which took place in a rural situation by contrast, was largely vernacular, with some translation of English into Kikuyu, and lasted 90 minutes.

80 *Account of St Matthew's Services* (Kirinyaga, 1996) in Morgan, 'Anglican Mission', pp 139ff.

3. *Music.*

The musical content of the Chrisco service was 100% European or American from the point of view of the origin of melodies, and nearly all were sung in English too, which may indicate the provenance of the church group or its leader, the preferred style of its members, or an international New Pentecostalist liturgical style.[81] Certainly there were no 'Swahili choruses', of the kind that are common to Anglican and East African Revival-style worship. The melodies of the Anglican service were 50% Euro-American, from an early hymn collection, but nearly all of these were sung in Kikuyu; the rest were both composed and sung in Kikuyu or Swahili, either from the new *Nyimbo* book, or from memory

4. *Sermon.*

Readings were in English at Chrisco, and in Kikuyu at St. Matthew's. The sermon was an important part of both liturgies, the Chrisco example using an Old Testament Exodus theme, which is one of the most popular texts for its leverage, according to John Mbiti. The Anglican sermon, translated into Kikuyu, was not as long but the service all together was longer. The importance that ACK ordinands place on preaching is the highest of a list of components of the liturgy which they were asked to place in order of importance.[82] It is highly respected as a form of devotional, social, prophetic and narrative communication, and it is not without significance that most churchmembers in Kenya would be expected to be able to stand and articulate their faith in delivering a 'testimony', and that a number of ordinands are former catechists or evangelists.

5. *Prayers.*

Although there was more led prayer and participative and simultaneous use of glossolalia[83] at Chrisco, the leadership of the prayers was from the worship-leader at the front, whilst at St. Matthew's different people came forward and participated. It may be that the call for Anglican worship to be more participative[84] refers to the perceived need for simultaneous personal pentecostal-style worship because the actual level of participation at the Anglican service was higher. There is evidence that an older generation appreciates the Kikuyu translation, which although more modern than Cranmer's prose, sounds strange to a younger ear.[85] Also noteworthy is that some younger Christians have been told by New Pentecostalist Christians that they cannot pray using a Prayer Book, since prayer

81 See in this respect Paul Gifford who analyzes the musical styles, as well as the 'Prosperity Theology' of these charismatic churches elsewhere in Africa: according to him the hymns are sometimes English translated into Ewe, sometimes into Akan, but always with western rhythms. 'Ghana's Charismatic Churches' in *Journal of Religion in Africa, XXIV Fasc.3*, (August 1994), pp 241-265; 'Prosperity: A New and Foreign Element in African Christianity' in *Religion 20*, (October 1990) pp 373-388.

82 See *Survey*, in Morgan, 'Anglican Mission', p 206ff.

83 Something which mainstream churches do not encourage, e.g. the MCK, *Interview* with Rt. Revd. Z. Nthamburi, (Nairobi, 1996), in Morgan, 'Anglican Mission', p 145.

84 See *Survey* in Morgan, 'Anglican Mission', p 206ff.

85 *Interviews*, including, Jeffithah Mugo, (Kirinyaga, 1996), in Morgan, 'Anglican Mission', p 145 .

must come from their heart (and even to throw their *BCP*s away.) Overall, however, there is general respect amongst Anglicans for the New Pentecostalist groups.[86]

6. Conclusion of Analysis

It can be seen that there are contrasting dynamics in the worship fields of both churches. Whilst the Pentecostal tendency is demonstrated in the Chrisco church, and there appears to be a freedom of expression in the liturgy, this is personal rather than public. The Anglican Church form, even the *BCP* structure, offers opportunities for a greater degree of participation, for example, someone to pray, someone to do the reading, indeed the office of Lay Reader, and the role of each of these is more clearly identified.

It would be wrong to equate the formality of the *BCP* structure with foreignness due to the high degree of indigenous music and the scope for participation in the Anglican liturgy, even if this is ritualized or needs to be legitimized by the authority. The latitude which the authority (that is, the Liturgical Commission) grants is considerable and under-exploited: Dr. Gitari has challenged many to formulate liturgies. Similarly, spontaneity cannot equate with contextuality; Joyce Karuri's Introduction to *Nyimbo* shows how much work was required to put the book together, and it is clear in this comparison that it is the music in the ACK which is more truly indigenous.

In brief it may be stated from the liturgical point of view that an Anglican *BCP* form, which is greatly appreciated by many ordinands, provides a framework to experience a variety of worship styles. Rigidity of form is a drawback in encouraging participation but it is often not the clergy but the lay readers who are conservative in these matters.[87] A most telling contrast between the individualistic New Pentecostal approach and the holistic communitarian approach to mission in the ACK is defined by the comment: 'we are here to bring individuals to Jesus, not communities.' The emphasis of mainstream Protestantism, accentuated in the *ACK* is precisely that only by doing the latter can the former be achieved.

Anglicanism would seem to be a theological and ecclesiological anachronism. But the socio-cultural field in many areas of Kenya has not been invested with capital in terms of a post-Enlightenment disenchantment with over-rationalistic philosophical categories.[88] The *ACK* thus appears not to be Western in a historical sense, but refreshingly post-modern, capable of being transformed, and of transforming, and it is experiencing, partly in common with other traditions, a particular inculturation.[89] Note this flexibility apparent in a Confirmation Service conducted by Dr. Gitari when he was Bishop of Kirinyaga. (See Appendix.)

86 *Interviews*, (SACTD, Kenya, 1996), in Morgan, 'Anglican Mission', p 145.

87 *Interview*, St. Paul's, Limuru Denominational Representatives, (Limuru, Kenya, 1996), in Morgan, 'Anglican Mission', p 145.

88 The Gambian American theologian, Lamin Sanneh sees 'the Enlightenment, the Romantic, and the Modern . . . cultural project' in Europe as an élitist alternative religion and wishes to propose a bottom-up re-evaluation of the theology indwelling cultures, L Sanneh, *Encountering the West*, (Marshall Pickering, London, 1993), p 24ff.

89 Alister McGrath speaks of Anglicanism 'gaining in strength where the Enlightenment has had a minimal impact' (*The Renewal of Anglicanism* (SPCK, London, 1993), p 18).

3

Aspects of Inculturation in Music, Drama and Protest

In sections One and Two I examined the contextualization of worship in particular church services. In this chapter I look at examples of liturgy as a tool in mission in relation to music, drama and protest.

Music

The Kikuyu hymn book, *Nyimbo Cia Gucanjamura Ngoro* (1995) produced by Revd Joyce Karuri and others can be seen as a contemporary illustration of continuity between the importance of music and dance evoked in the inculturation of the Revival hymns of the 1930's[90] and the marriage of theologically explicit text and local cultural forms. That the hymnbook has been encouraged, compiled and used in the area of ACK Diocese of Kirinyaga is a foremost example of contextualized worship, for in the Preface to the book Dr. Gitari notes that whilst singing outside the church is enthusiastic, entry into the building sometimes brings an unnecessarily solemn air. The creation of hymns for different occasions by Joyce Karuri and others, and usage of the Kikuyu hymn book is evidence of (episcopally-encouraged) grass-roots inculturation of worship drawing on secular or home-produced musical forms.

Examples from Nyimbo Cia Gucanjamura Ngoro, with translation and comment.

a. Hymn No. 211 *Twareheh Iheo Ciitũ* by Joyce Karuri Translation by Joyce Karuri verses 1-4 of 6 Key of E Flat Time 4/4

1. Twarehe iheo ciitũ rĩu Ngoro irĩ na ngatho (nyingĩ) Tũkiugaga nĩ wega Ngai Nĩgũtũrathima Twamũkĩre Mwathani O hamwe na indu ciitũ (baba) Ici twarehe mbere yaku Baba ciamũkĩre	1. We now present our gifts with gratitude in our hearts Saying 'thank you Lord for blessing us Accept us now Lord Together with the gifts that we bring before you Father accept them
2. Nikwagĩrĩĩre hingo ciothe Mũthenya wa kiumia (o kiumia) Tũrutage iheo ciitũ Cia wĩra wa Ngai	2. It's orderly that on every Sunday we come with gifts for the work of God
3. Amwe nĩmagaga kũruta Makoria nĩ ciakĩ (irutagwo) Magakĩĩgĩra mũthithũ Wa indo cia gũkũ thĩ	3. Some people refuse to give Wondering what it is for, And so they keep for themselves Worldly treasures

90 Historically, the discovery of traditional musical roots for worship has taken a long time in the Kenyan Anglican tradition. See J.E. Church's account of the East African revival, *Quest for the Highest, A Diary of the East African Revival* (Paternoster, Exeter, 1981), pp 131, 146; also, Paul van Thiel, 'African music in Christian worship' in *African Ecclesiastical Review* 3 (1) (February 1961) pp 73-76.

b. Hymn no. 215 *Nĩ Wega Ngai Mũtũũmbi* by Harrison Kathara and Peter Wanjohi
Verses 1-3 & 8 of 8 Key of E Time 5/8 3/8
chorus Nĩ wega Ngai mũtũũmbi
Nĩ gũtũmbira indo ingĩ nyingĩ
Ngai witũ tũgĩciona nĩ tuonaga hinya waku
Ona ningĩ nĩtũmatagia
Wĩtĩkio witũ

1. Twonaga gwatuka Ngai baba
tũkona gwathera nĩ-

2. Irĩma mĩkuru Ngai baba
nĩwe waciũmbire nĩ-

3. Nyamũ cia gĩthaka Ngai baba
nĩwe waciũmbire nĩ-

8. Mũthenya wa mũico Ngai Baba
Niwombire mũndũ nĩ-

No. 215 *Thank you O Lord our Creator*
(Translation by Joyce Karuri)
chorus Thank you God our Creator
For you have given us so much through creation
O God, when we look at all of them
we see your might, and our faith is further strengthened

1. We see the evening come, O God,
And then we see the dawn of a new day . . .

2. The hills and the valleys, you made them all . . .

3. The wildlife, O Father,
You are the one who created it . . .

8. And on the last day you created the human being . . .

Joyce Karuri writes that this is a very rich traditional melody which is a celebration of creation, and that worshippers enjoy singing it with great excitement.[91]

Drama

Drama and dialogue are often part of life in Kenya as the culture of *harambee* and *baraza*, a kind of response-led open-air political meeting[92], show. The Kenyan Anglican Youth Organisation (KAYO) is often a springboard for leadership within the ACK, and the popular expression of *the kesha*, a youth-led mixture of prayer, preaching and social activity in the context of a vigil, are evidence of the way in which young people are a leaven to the liturgical life of the church. A historical parallel is appropriate at this point.

A comparable example of the influence of young people and young clergy in contemporary African mission is the Passion play which two students at St Andrew's Institute (now SACTD), Pauline Njiru and Kabiro Gatumu[93] wrote in 1991. This was about the last week of Jesus' life with echoes of the then current events and political language of Kenya. Graham Kings wrote:

> 'Part of it was performed on Graduation Day, 12th October 1991. In August 1990, the prophetic Bishop Muge, had been threatened by Peter Okondo,

91 *Letter*, Revd J. Karuri, 11 August 2000.

92 *Baraza* may offer a stage on which state élites use political oratory to foster national unity, territorial identification, and loyalty to the ruling régime. Here we see the construction and diffusion of national culture: those "intentional élite products which draw on élite, folk, mass and popular forms, and use indigenous as well as cosmopolitan technologies of reproduction and dissemination".' (A.Haugerud, *The Culture of Politics in Modern Kenya*, (Cambridge, 1995), pp 57-8).

93 The Revd Kabiro Gatumu is currently engaged in research for a PhD in New Testament under the supervision of James Dunn, Professor of Divinity in the University of Durham, UK.

a cabinet minister, that if he "went to Busia he would see fire and may not leave alive". He went and died. A lorry smashed into his car on the way home. On Graduation Day, a shiver went through the crowd when Jesus was warned by the Sadducees "if you go to Jerusalem, you will see fire and may not leave alive."
'Another politician, Sharif Massir from Mombasa, caused a stir when he said that the queuing system of voting would be implemented "whether the people like it or not." In Kiswahili this neat catchphrase "wapende wasipende" became infamous. In the Passion Play the scene portraying the Sanhedrin Council deciding the fate of Jesus, concluded with the High Priest saying this: "I know the people are behind him, we will have to get rid of him- 'wapende wasipende.'" A gasp went up in the crowd.'[94]

Protest

The Kenyan constitution enshrines freedom of worship in consecrated buildings but a certain wariness prevails in relation to worship in other places. Many forms of worship have oral or narrative roots in a social setting, (birth, marriage, harvest, and so on), but they are made distinctive by synthesis with Christian theology. Political events in Kenya have been set in a liturgical context and that this has given legitimacy to social and political comment. Two examples will illustrate this point.

A few months before Kenya ceased to be a *de jure* one-party state in December 1991, a provocative article appeared in *The Weekly Review* entitled 'Running Out of Steam, The CPK seems to be in disarray over its political approach'[95]. At this time Dr. Gitari was at his rhetorical height, preaching and devising liturgy to challenge environmental exploitation and financial corruption in the government, not to mention the desirability of multi-partyism.[96] Archbishop Kuria had announced in mid-July that 'special prayers' for the return of peace and justice would be held in the cathedral and other churches on that day. The secretary of the CPK's Justice and Peace Commission announced that the prayer service would be preceded by a public procession through Nairobi's streets. Subsequently the government warned the public against attending the service and said it would not allow the procession to take place on account, the journalist argued, of the memory of a violent aftermath of an 'unlicensed prayer crusade' in Nyeri district, organized by Revd Timothy Njoya of the Presbyterian Church of East Africa (PCEA). There were reports of intimidation against senior CPK clergy and lawyers by security personnel.[97]

That such a scenario was viewed as so inimical by the government is revealing: church worship may happily draw on the social context in the state (that is, pray for national leaders) but uneasily comment in its worship on that social context. The prophetic role of liturgy is brought out further in the following example.

94 Graham Kings, 'Proverbial, Intrinsic and Dynamic Authorities', p 141.
95 *Weekly Review*, (2 August 1992) pp 3-6.
96 See 'Was there no Naboth to say no?'(19 May 1991) and 'You are Doomed, You Shepherds of Israel' (9 June 1991), in D Gitari, *In Season and Out of Season* (Regnum, Oxford, 1996), p 73ff.
97 *Weekly Review*, (Kenya, 2 August 1992) p 4.

Many found it disturbing to see Kenyan riot troops beating students and worshippers in All Saints Cathedral, an event which gained international news and television media coverage in 10-17 July 1997. Further unrest was reported particularly in Nakuru and deaths occurred elsewhere. Revd. Timothy Njoya, who had been injured himself, returned with others to the Cathedral in full sight of the foreign media for a 'cleansing ceremony'. Activists carried green branches to symbolize peace as Archbishop David Gitari sprinkled holy water and then knocked three times on the door to mark its reopening for services:

'Open the gates of this cathedral so that I may enter and cleanse it.'[98]

Gitari's sermon included an impassioned appeal for justice based on Daniel 5.1-13, declaring of President Moi: 'You have been weighed in the balance and found wanting.' The liturgy also included a litany for the security forces to be guided, protected and inspired.[99] The unpublished text of the sermon contains letters of support from Archbishops of other Provinces and a statement from an opposition MP. This successful public act provided a powerful link between prophetic and social engagement in the context of worship which was of international political importance.

4
African Origins, the Revival and the Book of Common Prayer

One of the factors giving power to the new services is the fact that they are—or that their participants are in a cultural sense—imbued with covenant theology, biblical and African titles for God, and Old Testament themes which are particularly appropriate for some ethnic groups in Kenya. These issues are worth examining in more detail in relation to the names of God since they will deepen an understanding of the dynamic of liturgy.

Titles for God

With regard to Old Testament and covenant theology, in the Communion service the confession is based, as has been noted above, on Genesis 1.27 and the absolution, on Psalm 103.11-12:

> 'Almighty God, Creator of all . . .
> we have corrupted ourselves and damaged your likeness . . .
> Almighty God, whose steadfast love is as great as the heavens are high above the earth, remove your sins from you as far as the east is from the west, . . .'[100]

Reference to the Almightiness, creating and sustaining power of God is made in

98 *Channel 4* television news (UK, 14 July 1997)
99 *The Guardian* news report (UK, 14 July 1997), p 12.
100 *KSHC*, pp 24-5

the *Modern Services*[101], and emphasized by the matrices of Scriptures offered as 'Introductory Sentences', for example:

> God rained down upon them manna to eat, and gave them the grain of heaven. *(Psalm 78.24)*[102]
>
> For with you is the well of life; and in your light shall we see light. (*Psalm 36.9)*
>
> ... Come, let us go to the mountain of the Lord that he may teach us his ways and that we may walk in his paths. (*Isaiah 2.)3* [103]

The reference to mountains is crucial to an understanding of some African traditional theology, as it is to understanding the establishment of the covenant at Sinai[104]. Traditionalist Kikuyu, for example, relate to four sacred mountains: *Kia-Njahi* (or *Kia-Ikamba*, Mountain of the Kamba), the Bean Mountain or *Kilimamboga*, *Kia-Mbiruiru* (the Blue-Black Mountain or *Ngong* Hills), *Kia-Nyandarua* (the *Kinangop* or Aberdares); *Kiriama-Kia-Ngai* (God's Mountain or *Longonot*), also called *Kiriama-Kia-Ihoro* (the Mountain with a hole) was not sacred. The most important is *Kiri-Nyaga* (Mount Kenya) for *Mwene-Nyaga* (God) had appeared there, mysteriously leaving snow at the summit; from there he brought *Gikuyu* and *Mumbi* into being according to the Creation myth. On these highest mountains the Owner of All descended, in Old Testament fashion, to view his property and to bring blessings and punishments; the snow on *Kiri-Nyaga* was a symbol of purity which was smeared on children and used in sacrifices.[105] Some attention to the names of God will help to focus the argument as this was crucial to the Old Testament covenantal scheme. (See, for example, Exodus 3.13ff.; 6.2ff)

The point has been well made that the many names for God do not connote a plurality of gods in any way. By an analysis of Swahili, Frankl has shown that the titles *Mugu* (Kiswahili) *EnkAi* (Kimaasai) and *Nyasaye* (Dholuo) are not three different gods but one God and that there are three different languages which 'in a post-Babel world reflect three different cultures but express one religious idea.'[106] Comparison of the names for God between the Kikuyu and the Kamba and the Maasai may be made as these groups neighbour the Kikuyu. For Kikuyu culture *Ngai* represented the greatest divider or provider; *Ngai Mumbi* was God the Creator, *Ngai Baba*, God the Father, and *Mwathani*, the distinctively eminent ruler of all, a term which is also used in the Christian sense of 'Lord.' Wachege draws attention to the name *Githuuri*, Unsurpassed Elder, which corresponds with the Johannine pre-existent Logos, and yet with a specific human dimension.[107] The

101 See also *Morning Prayer*, pp 23,26; *Evening Prayer*, p 42; see p 17 above

102 *KSHC* , p 2.

103 *Modern Services* pp 1-2

104 See biblical references to Mounts Sinai, Exodus 19, 24, 34; Horeb, (the giving of the Ten Commandments to Moses), Deut 5-10; Mounts Gerizim and Ebal (blessings and curses), Deut 11.

105 P N Wachege, *Jesus Christ, Our Muthamaki (Ideal Elder)* (Phoenix, Nairobi, 1992), pp 49-50.

106 P J L Frankl, 'The Word for "God" in Swahili' in *Journal of Religion in Africa*, Vol XXV, Fasc.2, (May 1995), pp 202-211.

107 This was so because: *niwe wa tene na tene. Aari ho kuuma tene na egutura tene na tene-* He is of long ago. He has been in being and he will last everlastingly. (cf. For biblical comparison, see Rev. 1.4b) This is a link in Wachege's argument for Christ as the *Muthamaki*; see P N Wachege, *Jesus Christ our Muthamaki*, p 47.

Kamba called God *Mwatuangi* (Cleaver, distributor) and *Asa* (Father) as well as *Mulungu, Ngai* and *Mumbi* (Creator, Maker, Fashioner). The Maasai have a great number of names for God. Here are a few of them: *Enkai* as the Originator, *Emayian*, the One who blesses, and *Pasai, Parsai*, 'One prayed to "O, God."'[108] The Turkana, on the other hand, as a nomadic group, appear to have a slightly different concept of God as *Akuj*, a Source-Being. It is a particularly immanent idea of God who exists in spirits and then particularly in the old.[109] The waso-Boorana, a similar group, have a dynamic concept of the deity also; they believe that God is one and speaks different languages so that the God of the Borana in Ethiopia, the God of Islam, and the God of Christianity are the same. A scholar has pointed out that they view the eagle particularly as a transmitter of God's will, and construct rites around its appearance on their landscapes.[110] In these liturgies the interface with Islam is particularly relevant, a factor which is important also in relation to the Gabbra ethnic group who are cousins to the Borana.

The first Anglican bishops of Nakuru and Mount Kenya, Neville Langford-Smith and Obadiah Kariuki were adherents of the East African Revival Movement. Constraints of space preclude a thorough examination of the liturgical impact of the Revival here, but the impact was conceptual rather than textual. Max Warren wrote of the esteem in which the Book of Common Prayer (BCP*)*, along with the Bible, is held in the Movement, a fact which is underlined by Dr. Gitari and others.[111] This present writer argues that the crucifixion and stoic themes of many East African Revival conventions have resonated with the sombre, Christological and penitential tone of the BCP. The content and faith of the BCP which was created by an individual for a people at a particular time has achieved, by its translation and use, a transcendence in the spiritual lives of many (now) older African and Kenyan Christians who are also Revival adherents so that it became a basis for ongoing mission and for current liturgical developments. The catechisms learnt by baptism candidates or confirmands, and taught by evangelists are ingrained in many Christian leaders at present. The formalism of the BCP has been the foundation for much internalized theology and the source of some frustration due to concern amongst many clergy in the Kenyan dioceses under scrutiny, as new Pentecostal churches are drawing many young people to them.[112]

The tragic irony of the fact that one of the greatest periods of bloodletting in recent East African history took place in a nation (Rwanda) most deeply marked by Revival is investigated elsewhere.[113] This turn of events is an incentive to seek harmony in diversity and to allow ecumenism and careful theological inculturation

108 Doug Priest Jr., *Doing Theology with the Maasai*, (William Carey Library, Pasadena, 1990), p 115.

109 K v d Jagt, *The Religion of the Turkana of Kenya, An Anthropological Study*, (Elinkwijk, Utrecht, 1983.)

110 Mario I Aguilar, 'The eagle as messenger, pilgrim and voice: divinatory processes among the waso-Boorana of Kenya' in *Journal of Religion in Africa*, V.XXVII, Fas. *1*, (Feb. 96), pp 56-72. See Donovan's classic account of the Maasai where he discovers that the Lion has an important place in their understanding of the deity, *Christianity Rediscovered, An Epistle from the Maasai*, (Orbis, NY, 1978).

111 *Interview* with Revd Shadrach Mwangangi, Tutor, Berea College of Theology, Diocese of Nakuru, December 1995, in Morgan, 'Anglican Mission', p 59.

112 *Interview*, Mwangangi, in Morgan, 'Anglican Mission', p 60; and *Survey* in Morgan, p 206ff.

113 Roger Bowen, 'Rwanda—Missionary Reflections on a Catastrophe, J C Jones Lecture 1995' in *Anvil*, 13, No. 1, (1996), pp 33-44.

to immunize a society against any possible recurrence of this. Theological and liturgical education are important in this process.

Terry Ranger has spoken of the defect of early Christian mission historiography (in East, Central or Southern Africa) as underplaying the cultural and religious aspects whilst expanding on the political and economic, since 'formal church historians, writing from within the missionary societies, have emphasized institutional achievements, the build-up of schools and clinics, and have hardly discussed the impact of missionaries and their African catechists on the cultural imagination.' [114]

This problem has been addressed, as noted above, by Kenyan theologians such as John Karanja and Gideon Githige.[115] Karanja points out the influence of the 'highly innovative and adaptive culture' of the Kikuyu and identifies 'the extent to which the Kikuyu Anglican Church was indebted to indigenous models and experiences for its impetus, dynamism and direction.'[116] The marriage of the symbolism of Kikuyu ritual and Christianity provided a rich and various field with political and ethnic implications:

> 'Christianity and the Bible gave the Kikuyu God, *Ngai*, a past which was longer and more precise than the mists of *tene na agu* (a named generation) . . . *Ngai* became Jehovah, a tribal and interventionist God, father of a people whom he repeatedly rescued from the hand of their enemies. In the minds of Kikuyu people the Bible fostered a Kikuyu tribe.'[117]

These facts were particularly pertinent in the development of a Kikuyu Anglican Church in the Central Province, with its indebtedness to Kikuyu indigenous social and ritual models. Githige paints in the details of political development, noting the influence of the church as in conservative, in relation to extreme politics, and progressive, in relation to a colonialist church past.

The importance of social context in mission became clearer during the post-colonial era and bible translation and liturgical production were part of this process. The impetus for inculturation in the liturgy came from Roman Catholic and Independent churches, but the CPK had its particular approach. In 1975 mission and social responsibility were being reflected upon by evangelical Anglican Christians after the Lausanne Conference of 1974. Also the momentum of liturgical change was increasing in Kenya: at the beginning of the 1970s a prototype modernization of the 1662 BCP was produced[118]; an attempt was made to 'simplify the liturgy at the centre of the lives of Christians and make it more meaningful in the CPK.'[119] In the 1970s, therefore, a translation of the archaic

114 Terence Ranger, 'Religious Movements and Politics in Sub-Saharan Africa' in *African Studies Review*, 29, No.2, (1986) p 35.

115 Gideon Githige, 'The Church as the bulwark against extremism: development of Church and State relations in Kenya with particular reference to the years after political independence 1963-1992, Ph.D.', Open University/Oxford Centre for Mission Studies, 1997. John K Karanja, 'The Growth of the African Anglican Church in Central Kenya, 1900-1945', Ph.D, Faculty of History, University of Cambridge, April 1993, (published-Nairobi: Uzima, 1999).

116 Karanja, 'The Growth of the African Anglican Church' , p 3.

117 Bruce Berman and John Lonsdale (eds), *Unhappy Valley*, p 354.

118 *Written comment*, Dr Kevin Ward, Teacher in Kenya, 1969-71, 5 February 1996, in Morgan, 'Anglican Mission', p 3 .

English into readable English was authorized in an orange booklet called *Modern English Services*.[120] In 1975 also, the Presbyterian Church published their *Church Service Book* written in English but based on services originally prepared in Kikuyu. In the 1980s the CPK Provincial Synod established a liturgical committee out of the previous liturgical commission to continue the process which had begun.

5
Kenyan Liturgies: Work in Progress

In a society as multi-ethnic as Kenya, should services be written in English rather than in the vernacular, Kiswahili, or in other local languages. English is the language? of education, government and law, however, and as such now carries with it few colonialist overtones. Although the *KSHC* was written in English, it was both intended for translation, and also encompassed different cultural expressions translated as it were from their original contexts. This is so for other liturgies, too.

KSHC was compiled at the instigation of Dr Gitari, then Bishop of Kirinyaga, and Chairman of the Liturgical Commission and was edited by Graham Kings who contributed both to *KSHC* and *Modern Services*. Writers in the ACK such as the Rt Rev Gideon Githige, the Ven Sam Mawiyoo, Rev Joyce Karuri and Rev John Nyesi have added increased value to the project in recent years.

Current Liturgies

In Nakuru diocese a number of liturgies were being collected at an informal level and a Committee of Writers of Important Topics and Liturgies was discharged with the responsibility of compiling them. The following were listed:

Unveiling of the Cross; Blessing of a Christian House; Thanksgiving Services (for passing exams, for the purchase of a vehicle, for buying a shamba (farm), harvest); Blessing of a Civil Wedding; Inductions of an Archdeacon and of a Rural Dean; Admitting of KAYO, Mothers' Union and Fathers' Association Members; Commissioning of Boys and Girls Brigades; Blessing of the Lord's Acre[121]; Receiving Members from Other Denominations; Admitting Layreaders.[122]

These were created by clergy in the parishes with the encouragement of the Provincial Liturgical Committee and were to be passed up to PBTE level for ratification. Meanwhile they are being used and developed at the ground level and will eventually go into a manual for use in the diocese. There was in 1996, for example, no provincial consensus on the liturgy for admitting layreaders so each diocese would have had its own procedures. This situation is currently being addressed.

119 The Provincial Unit of Research, CPK, *Rabai to Mumias, A Short History of the Church of the Province of Kenya, 1844-1944*, (Uzima, Nairobi, 1994), pp 165-6

120 See note 10. The *Modern English Services* contained *Morning and Evening Prayer, Baptism of Children, Baptism of Adults*, and *Holy Communion*.

121 An area of private land which is set aside so that the produce from it is sold to benefit the church's work.

122 Ven. Paul Ngure, *Interview*, Archdeacon of Biharti, Nakuru, 2 March 1996, in Morgan, 'Anglican Mission', p 174. Sad to relate, the Ven. Paul Ngure died in a car crash.

There is thus evidence of creativity and innovation in the area of liturgy in the CPK/ACK and this is a fulfillment of the wish of the Liturgical Commission and the present Archbishop.

In the last few years the ACK formed an Alternative Prayer Book Committee, of which the Ven Sam Mawiyoo is the Chairman, and Rev Joyce Karuri was appointed the Provincial Editor in October 1999. Their mandate is to complete the new ACK Prayer Book and the Indigenous Sacred Hymnal. Much work has been done and the present target date is Easter 2002. At present the Confirmation and Admission to Communion services from *Modern Services* are already being used experimentally. Overall, many people are involved in this project which will involves a review of the existing *KSHC* and *Modern Services* and the inclusion of 15 new services:

Holy Matrimony; Blessing of Marriage; Burial of a Christian/Still Born/Infant; Making of Deacons; Ordination of Priests; Consecration of a Bishop; Reconciliation of a Penitent; Dedication and Consecration of a Church; Thanksgiving after Child Birth/Adoption; Laying the Foundation Stone of a Church/Building; Prayer for a Church Site/a Burial Yard; Baptism- Emergency & Conditional; A Litany & the Psalter; Catechism; Visitation to the Sick/Service of Healing[123]

In addition to these, the Committee is considering orders for the Reaffirmation/ Renewal of Marriage Vows, the Licensing of Layreaders, the Commissioning of Evangelists/Catechists, Night Prayer (Second Order), a Service of Thanksgiving after a Life-threatening Experience, a Service of Thanksgiving after a Harvest, and one for the Restoration of Things Profaned. The Litany for the Preservation of the Environment is also being incorporated into the work as well as prayers for various purposes and a Catechism.[124]

The draft contains many litanies, prayers which have been specially composed and from elsewhere. It is rich in responsorial material, biblical quotations and references, and the placing of hymns and songs. In relation to these developments it may be truly said that:

> '[The influence of the Old Prayer Book] is waning, though a recognizably Anglican worshipping character persists. Yet this needs to be consciously sustained, expressed, renewed, and re-expressed'[125].

Alongside this can be placed the view of Mbonigaba underlining the perception of Holeton that 'the first generation of indigenous leaderships tends to cling closely to the inherited liturgical tradition and with reluctance strays from BCP 1662.'[126] It is this generation that the ACK has left behind; it was in fact at the CPK residential conference on liturgy in April 1991 in Kabare, that Kenyan Anglicans were observed to have loosened their attachment to the 1662 rite.[127]

123 The Ven Sam Mawiyoo, *Letter*, 28 August 2000.

124 *New ACK Prayer Book Draft*, Anglican Church of Kenya, 2000.

125 *Many Gifts, One Spirit- Report of ACC-7: Singapore 1987*, (Church House Publishing, London, 1987), p 75, cited in *News of Liturgy*, No. 153 (September 1987), p 7.

126 E.Mbonigaba quoting from an *Unpublished Paper* by David Holeton (1988), in 'The Indigenization of Liturgy' in Gitari, *Anglican Inculturation*, 1994.

127 Colin Buchanan writing on receiving *Modern Services* materials, in *News of Liturgy*, No. 199, (July 1991) p 9.

Conclusion

The Ven Sam Mawiyoo records that translations have so far only been completed into Kiswahili for *KSHC* and *Modern Services*. The publishers, Uzima Press, report sales of 33,000 copies of *KSHC* during the ten-year period (1989-1999), 31,549 being purchased in Kenya; sales of *Modern Services* (1991-2000) amounted to 41,500, 40,844 being bought in Kenya. Translations are to be carried out once all the liturgies have been authorized. Cultural differences exist in that certain scriptural applications prove not to be acceptable for some local uses. The overall aim is translate the entirety of the book rather than individual services once it is agreed and to that end drafts have been sent to dioceses for simultaneous experimentation.[128] However, Mawiyoo continues, non-written liturgies also happen spontaneously which are not translated since they are situational.[129] Joyce Karuri stresses the importance of leaving room for creativity and announces that other useful liturgies are likely to be published in another booklet. This is an indication of the openness of Kenyan Anglican culture to a form of worship which integrates the sacred into the everyday.

In the Preface to this Study the Archbishop of the ACK, Dr. David Gitari, writes that the fruits of the new Kenyan prayer book are eagerly awaited. It is conceivable that those committed to the process of Western liturgical renewal are only just awakening to the possibilities which liturgical dynamism in other parts of the world, namely Africa, represent. We are all learning from the insights of the worship of *Yahweh*, of *Ngai*, of the living God, that culture-sensitive (and, however surprisingly, Anglican) liturgies are not only descriptive but also performative and instrumental in mission. Dr. Gitari also refers to a 'foretaste', which is a most apt expression of the many flavours of the worship of heaven which we hope that this study points to, and which will surely be more widely experienced with the production of the new Kenyan Anglican prayer book.

128 Joyce Karuri, Letter.
129 Mawiyoo, Letter.

Appendix

Snapshot Three : *Analysis of a Confirmation Service conducted by Rt Rev Dr David Gitari in Giriama, Kirinyaga diocese, 10.00-12.00 on 25 Febrary 1996.*

Within the context of the BCP Order of Confirmation the Bishop endeavoured to make what he called afterwards a 'rather dull order', more interesting. The sense of occasion was firstly heightened by the women, or Mothers' Union with white headscarves, and the 'People's Wardens' wearing special uniforms although the 'Vicars' Wardens', who are traditionally the Vice-Chairmen of the PCCs, did not. 2 evangelists, who were involved in preparing the candidates (none of whom are under 13) for confirmation, presented the 80 people to the bishop. The service began with the rehearsal of the Catechism, or a version of it, from the BCP, with all candidates responding with the full text learnt by heart, including the Creed and Ten Commandments. After the confirmation of the adults, parents and godparents were invited to stand up, with the acknowledgement by the bishop that many had travelled a long way, and asked to accompany the young people to the altar rail, two at a time. The young people knelt, were prayed for, and then welcomed by their parents and godparents to the family of the church. Then all the confirmed came into the chancel and were greeted amidst much joyful singing. After this the bishop blessed all 34 babies and gave them permission to be noisy in church and reprimanded wardens for occasions when he knew they had not 'suffered little children' but peremptorily asked them to leave.

The bishop led the singing of the hymn, 'How Great Thou art' and encouraged people to call out names of birds, trees etc.; some people had traditional animal names: Messrs. 'Giraffe' and 'Frog' were to stand up; we turned to one another and stated: 'You are made in the image of God.' The bishop then preached on the theme of stewardship of God's natural, spiritual and environmental gifts: before the sermon a group of schoolgirls had begged the bishop to hear an extra of their beautifully-harmonized songs; he asked: where are the men, are they not given the gift of singing? He castigated religious and political defectors: so many people go from one denomination to another, 'CPK' one day, a Pentecostalist the next, that they will be in danger of missing the kingdom of God. The opposition politicians who were changing back to supporting the official KANU party were letting us all down because they were being swayed by a different 'wind of doctrine', that of money and bribery. After the service a significant time was spent outside the church reinforcing the points made (the dangers of selling tea and coffee to unauthorized private outlets), distributing gifts and in prayer. In an interview with a newspaper reporter after the service the bishop said that it would be impossible to go back to a one-party system now, and that if that was the tendency church leaders would have to re-occupy their position as the quasi-political opposition as they had done in that era.[130]

130 Morgan, 'Anglican Mission', p 208.

THE GROUP FOR RENEWAL OF WORSHIP (GROW)

This Group, originally founded in 1961, has for thirty years taken responsibility for the Grove Books publications on liturgy and worship. Its membership and broad aims reflect a highly reforming, pastoral and missionary interest in worship. Beginning with a youthful evangelical Anglican membership in the early 1970s, the Group has not only probed adventurously into the future of Anglican worship, but has also with growing sureness of touch taken its place in promoting weighty scholarship. Thus the list of 'Grove Liturgical Studies' (on page 56) shows how, over a twelve-year period, the quarterly Studies added steadily to the material available to students of patristic, reformation and modern scholarly issues in liturgy. In 1986 the Group was approached by the Alcuin Club Committee with a view to publishing the new series of Joint Liturgical Studies, and this series is, at the time of writing, in its fifteenth year of publication, sustaining the programme with three Studies each year, and reaching its half-century with this Study.

Between the old Grove Liturgical Studies and the new Joint Liturgical Studies there is a large provision of both English language texts and other theological works on the patristic era. A detailed consolidated list is available from the publishers.

Since the early 1970s the Group has had Colin Buchanan as chairman and Trevor Lloyd as vice-chairman.

THE ALCUIN CLUB

The Alcuin Club exists to promote the study of Christian liturgy in general, and in particular the liturgies of the Anglican Communion. Since its foundation in 1897 it has published over 130 books and pamphlets. Members of the Club receive some publications of the current year free and others at a reduced rate.

Information concerning the annual subscription, applications for membership and lists of publications is obtainable from the Treasurer, The Revd. T. R. Barker, The Parsonage, 8 Church Street, Spalding, Lincs. PE11 2 PB. (Tel. 01775 722675).

The Alcuin Club has an arrangement with the Liturgical Press, Collegeville, whereby the old tradition of an annual Alcuin Club major scholarly study has been restored. The first title under this arrangement was published in early 1993: Alastair McGregor, *Fire and Light: The Symbolism of Fire and Light in the Holy Week Services*. The second was Martin Dudley, *The Collect in Anglican Liturgy;* the third is Gordon Jeanes, *The Day has Come! Easter and Baptism in Zeno of Verona;* the fourth is Christopher Irvine (ed.), *They Shaped our Worship.*

The Joint Liturgical Studies were reduced to three per annum from 1992, and the Alcuin Club subscription now includes the annual publication (as above) and the three Joint Liturgical Studies. The full list of Joint Liturgical Studies is printed opposite. All titles but nos. 4 and 16 are in print.

Alcuin/GROW Joint Liturgical Studies

All cost £4.95 (US $8) in 2001—nos. 4 and 16 are out of print

1. **(LS 49) Daily and Weekly Worship—from Jewish to Christian** by Roger Beckwith
2. **(LS 50) The Canons of Hippolytus** edited by Paul Bradshaw
3. **(LS 51) Modern Anglican Ordination Rites** edited by Colin Buchanan
4. **(LS 52) Models of Liturgical Theology** by James Empereur
5. **(LS 53) A Kingdom of Priests: Liturgical Formation of the Laity: The Brixen Essays** edited by Thomas Talley
6. **(LS 54) The Bishop in Liturgy: an Anglican Study** edited by Colin Buchanan
7. **(LS 55) Inculturation: the Eucharist in Africa** by Phillip Tovey
8. **(LS 56) Essays in Early Eastern Initiation** edited by Paul Bradshaw,
9. **(LS 57) The Liturgy of the Church in Jerusalem** by John Baldovin
10. **(LS 58) Adult Initiation** edited by Donald Withey
11. **(LS 59) 'The Missing Oblation': The Contents of the Early Antiochene Anaphora** by John Fenwick
12. **(LS 60) Calvin and Bullinger on the Lord's Supper** by Paul Rorem

13-14 **(LS 61) The Liturgical Portions of the Apostolic Constitutions: A Text for Students** edited by W. Jardine Grisbrooke (This double-size volume costs double price (i.e. £9.90))

15 **(LS 62) Liturgical Inculturation in the Anglican Communion** edited by David Holeton

16. **(LS 63) Cremation Today and Tomorrow** by Douglas Davies
17. **(LS 64) The Preaching Service—The Glory of the Methodists** by Adrian Burdon
18. **(LS 65) Irenaeus of Lyon on Baptism and Eucharist** edited with Introduction, Translation and Commentary by David Power
19. **(LS 66) Testamentum Domini** edited by Grant Sperry-White
20. **(LS 67) The Origins of the Roman Rite** edited by Gordon Jeanes
21. **The Anglican Eucharist in New Zealand 1814-1989** by Bosco Peters

22-23 **Foundations of Christian Music: The Music of Pre-Constantinian Christianity** by Edward Foley (double-sized volume at £9.90)

24. **Liturgical Presidency** by Paul James
25. **The Sacramentary of Sarapion of Thmuis: A Text for Students** edited by Ric Lennard-Barrett
26. **Communion Outside the Eucharist** by Phillip Tovey
27. **Revising the Eucharist: Groundwork for the Anglican Communion** edited by David Holeton
28. **Anglican Liturgical Inculturation in Africa** edited by David Gitari

29-30. **On Baptismal Fonts: Ancient and Modern** by Anita Stauffer (double-sized volume at £9.90)

31. **The Comparative Liturgy of Anton Baumstark** by Fritz West
32. **Worship and Evangelism in Pre-Christendom** by Alan Kreider
33. **Liturgy in Early Christian Egypt** by Maxwell E. Johnson
34. **Welcoming the Baptized** by Timothy Turner
35. **Daily Prayer in the Reformed Tradition: An Initial Survey** by Diane Karay Tripp
36. **The Ritual Kiss in Early Christian Worship** by Edward Phillips
37. **'After the Primitive Christians': The Eighteenth-century Anglican Eucharist in its Architectural Setting** by Peter Doll
38. **Coronations Past, Present and Future** edited by Paul Bradshaw
39. **Anglican Orders and Ordinations** edited by David Holeton
40. **The Liturgy of St James as presently used** edited by Phillip Tovey
41. **Anglican Missals** by Mark Dalby
42. **The Origins of the Roman Rite vol 2** edited by Gordon Jeanes
43. **Baptism in Early Byzantine Palestine 325-451** by Juliette Day
44. **Ambrosianum Mysterium: the Church of Milan and its Liturgical Tradition Vol. 1** by Cesare Alzati (translated by George Guiver)
45. **Mar Nestorius and Mar Theodore the Interpreter: the Forgotten Eucharistic Prayers of East Syria** edited by Bryan Spinks
46. **The Eucharistic Theology of the Later Nonjurors** by James Smith

47-48. **Ambrosianum Mysterium: the Church of Milan and its Liturgical Tradition Vol. II** by Cesare Alzati (translated by George Guiver) (double-sized volume at £9.90)

49. **The Syriac Version of the Liturgy of St James: A brief history for Students** by Dr Baby Varghese
50. **Offerings from Kenya to Anglicanism: Liturgical Texts and Contents including 'A Kenyan Service of Holy Communion'** by Graham Kings and Geoff Morgan

Grove Liturgical Studies

This series began in March 1975, and was published quarterly until 1986. Each title has 32 or 40 pages. No's 1, 3-6, 9, 10, 16, 30, 33, 36, 44 and 46 are out of print. Asterisked numbers have been reprinted. Prices in 2001. £2.75.

*2 **LANGUAGE LITURGY AND MEANING** by Anthony Thiselton

*7 **WHAT DID CRANMER THINK HE WAS DOING?** by Colin Buchanan

*8 **HIPPOLYTUS: A Text for students with translation, notes and commentary** by Geoffrey J. Cuming

11 **USING THE BIBLE IN WORSHIP** edited by Christopher Byworth

*12/13 **WORSHIP IN THE NEW TESTAMENT** by C. F. D. Moule (80 pages, £5 (US$11))

14 **THE END OF THE OFFERTORY: An Anglican Study** by Colin Buchanan

15 **ESSAYS ON HIPPOLYTUS** edited by Geoffrey Cuming

17 **AUTHORITY AND FREEDOM IN THE LITURGY** edited by Kenneth Stevenson

18 **CHARLES SIMEON, PREACHER EXTRAORDINARY** by Hugh Evan Hopkins

19 **EUCHARISTIC OFFERING IN THE EARLY CHURCH** by Richard P. C. Hanson (28 pages)

20 **THE DEVELOPMENT OF THE NEW EUCHARISTIC PRAYERS IN THE CHURCH OF ENGLAND** edited by Colin Buchanan

21 **THE WESTMINSTER DIRECTORY OF PUBLIC WORSHIP** with an introduction by Ian Breward

22 **E. C. RATCLIFF: REFLECTIONS ON LITURGICAL REVISION** edited by David H. Tripp

23 **SYMBOLISM AND THE LITURGY (I)** edited by Kenneth Stevenson

24 **ADDAI AND MARI—THE ANAPHORA OF THE APOSTLES: A TEXT FOR STUDENTS** edited by Bryan Spinks

25 **MAKING THE LITURGICAL PSALTER** by David Frost

26 **SYMBOLISM AND THE LITURGY (II)** edited by Kenneth Stevenson

27 **INFANT COMMUNION—THEN AND NOW** by David Holeton

28 **HE GAVE THANKS: AN INTRODUCTION TO THE EUCHARISTIC PRAYER** by Geoffrey Cuming

29 **THE LITURGICAL PORTIONS OF THE DIDASCALIA** edited by Sebastian Brook and Michael Vasey

31 **EUCHARISTIC SACRIFICE—THE ROOTS OF A METAPHOR** by Rowan Williams

32 **WHOSE OFFICE? DAILY PRAYER FOR THE PEOPLE OF GOD** by David Cutts and Harold Miller

*34 **EUCHARISTIC LITURGIES OF EDWARD VI: A Text for Students** edited by Colin Buchanan

35 **BACKGROUND DOCUMENTS TO LITURGICAL REVISION 1547-1549** edited by Colin Buchanan

37 **WHY LITURGICAL WORSHIP ANYWAY?** by Michael Sansom

38 **THE LITURGY OF THE FRANKFURT EXILES 1555** edited by Robin Leaver

39 **LATEST LITURGICAL REVISION IN THE CHURCH OF ENGLAND 1978-1984** by Colin Buchanan

40 **ESSAYS ON EUCHARISTIC SACRIFICE IN THE EARLY CHURCH** edited by Colin Buchanan

41 **ANGLICAN EUCHARISTIC LITURGY 1975-1985** by Colin Buchanan

*42 **A LITURGICAL GLOSSARY** compiled by Michael Sansom

43 **LITURGIES OF THE SPANISH AND PORTUGUESE REFORMED EPISCOPAL CHURCHES** edited by Colin Buchanan

45 **FOURTH CENTURY ANAPHORAL CONSTRUCTION TECHNIQUES** by John Fenwick

47 **THE MEDIEVAL GROWTH OF LITURGICAL SYMBOLISM** by Paul Rorem

*48 **ANGLICAN CONFIRMATION** by Colin Buchanan